Le… Your Place … p on the Couch with Snifters of Warm Brandy. You Begin to

WHISPER IN HIS EAR:

I had a sexy dream last night. And you were the *star!* In the dream I was a little taller, with jet-black hair, and was working in your campaign for the U.S. Senate. One night we had stayed late at campaign headquarters. When you invited me to take a spin in your new speedboat, I instantly accepted, and we were soon zooming across a beautiful mountain lake in the moonlight. While you drove the boat with one hand, you put the other around my shoulder. To your delight, you could feel my . . . breasts beneath my dress, but you were in for an even bigger surprise because I had slipped off my panties and tossed them into the boat's wake. I asked you to stop the boat so I could take a swim. I hadn't brought my bikini and so I proposed we skinny-dip. Swiftly, I pulled my dress over my head . . . I turned and dove into the water, swimming around the boat . . . Later we made love with the waves gently rocking the boat . . .

LIANE GARDNER

Whisper in His Ear

Futura

A Futura Book

This edition published in 1985
by Futura Publications, a Division of
Macdonald & Co (Publishers) Ltd
London & Sydney

ISBN 0 7088 2838 8

Printed and bound in Great Britain by
Collins, Glasgow

Futura Publications
A Division of
Macdonald & Co (Publishers) Ltd
Maxwell House
74 Worship Street
London EC2A 2EN

A BPCC plc Company

To Willie—

For being my inspiration,
Insisting on the challenge,
Showering me with precious love and affection,
And for the rewards I receive when I
Whisper in His Ear

Acknowledgments

Because of the nature of the material contained in this book I cannot publicly thank many of the people to whom I owe a debt of gratitude. Even if I were to refer to first names only, there would be speculation and possibly embarrassment for my friends and others who shared their intimate fantasy-stories with me.

However, I would like to thank my editor at Pocket Books, Sydny Miner, for having the courage to publish this book. And my beloved Willie has been the kindest, most supportive friend and lover any author could be lucky enough to have.

Finally, there is Michael, my agent, personal editor, and yes, my friend. Michael Snell has been with me throughout the conception, sale and many drafts of this book. He helped mold my ideas, challenged me time and again, and patiently edited draft after draft until, finally, the project found its way to completion. When the going got tough, Michael got tougher, yet he edited with a velvet glove. So thank you, Michael, Willie, Sydny, and everyone else who helped. And to my readers, whom I hope will finish this book with a wink and a smile, happy fantasies!

Liane Gardner
Anoopanadoon
November 17, 1983

Contents

Foreword 15

LESSON 1

Whispering in His Ear or The Art of Aural Sex 19

Are You Ready for Erotic Stories? / 20
Adding the Romantic Touches / 22
The Brain: The Most Powerful Sexual Organ / 23
How to Release the Little Boy in Your Man / 23
The Difference Between Fantasies and Fantasy Stories / 26
Overcoming Stage Fright / 26
Unleashing Your Own Powerful Sex Drive / 27
Fantasy Stories and the Liberated Woman / 27
Exercise 1: Popular Fantasies / 29

LESSON 2

Acting School 30

Homework the Teacher Never Assigned / 32
The Other Woman / 32
Men Love Women Who Ask Questions / 33
Learning How to Be an Investigative Reporter / 34
Clues / 35
Your Man's Sexual Fantasy Inventory / 35
Fleshing Out the Story! / 41
Using the Inventory to Create a Story / 44
Exercise 2: Creating Your First Fantasy Script / 47

LESSON 3

Tryouts 49

Ladies *Do* Talk Dirty / 52
Exercise 3: Required Reading / 54
Deliciously Dirty / 54
Tricks and Treats / 55
Sexual Assertiveness Training / 56
Cotton Undies Are for Nuns / 57
More Tricks and Treats / 57
Love Sounds / 58
Exercise 4: The Pillowtalk Game / 59
Training Your Voice / 61
Learning to Be a Spellbinder / 62
Exercise 5: An S.A.T. They Never Gave in High School / 65

LESSON 4

Off Broadway 69

Teasing Your Audience / 70
Slow and Easy / 71
Mildly Seasoned / 74
Wild and Wonderful / 79
The Male Animal / 80
Lighting the Slow Fuse / 81
Lighting a Shorter Fuse / 83
Dynamite / 85
Eliminating His Fears / 87
Tease, Then Please / 88

LESSON 5

Opening Night 89

When the Irresistible Force Meets an Immovable Object / 91
Searching for Buried Treasure: Fantasy Sources / 94
Props, Costumes, and Decorations / 97
What If Your Man Gets Too Excited? / 103
Marking That Magic Moment / 104
Blowing Your Man's Mind Without Lifting a Finger / 104
Sooner or Later I'm Gonna Getcha! / 105
Persistence Pays / 106
Exercise 6: Memorizing Those Magic Moments / 109

LESSON 6

Hit Show! 109

Clues That Signal a Need to Advance / 111
Keeping Your Budding Romance from Losing Its Bloom / 112
Paste-up Material / 114
Costumes / 115
Props / 117
Photography / 118
Video / 120
Publicity / 122
Computer Softpornware / 122

LESSON 7

Earning Your X-Rating 124

Strong Medicine / 125
Picking Your First Apple / 126
When You're Good You're Great, but When You're Bad You're Better! / 129
Group Sex While the Whole World Watches / 130
Voyeurism and the Family / 135
Playing Dress-up / 137
Dedicated to Nursing Mothers / 139
Turning the Tables / 140
Exercise 7: Fill in the Blanks / 140
Exercise 8: Now He's the Director / 142

LESSON 8

Sequels 143

Step One: Getting Your Man to Volunteer Clues / 145
Step Two: He Feeds Your Fantasies / 152
Loosen Their Tongues / 153
Your Own Sexual Fantasy Inventory / 155
A Brief Peek at Whisper in *Her* Ear / 157
Confiding Your Deepest, Darkest Secrets / 160
Real Women Love Flowers, Chocolates, and Mushy Cards / 161
Exercise 9: The Whisper in His Ear Game / 166

Foreword

I had been reading Jerzy Kosinski's *Pinball* the day before I planned to seduce a man. In the book, a beautiful music student develops an ingenious plan to ensnare a famous rock star.

The heroine, Andrea, decided to tease her idol until he would break down brick walls to get her. She listened to the man's music carefully, eliciting from the lyrics clues that revealed his secret life: he loved bullfights, adored Mexico, and wrote passionately about dark-eyed Latin beauties.

Having done her homework, Andrea wrote a series of increasingly erotic letters to her unsuspecting target, gradually worming her way into his fantasy life until he would do anything to meet her. Could I achieve similar power over my man? Well, the next night I got my chance, and the results changed my life.

We returned to Ryan's apartment after a romantic candlelit dinner to which I wore my most slinky and revealing dress. I noticed a stack of *Penthouse* and *Hustler* magazines piled high on the table near his bed. A well-worn collection of *Forum*, nearly a foot high, cluttered his bathroom. Hanging from its strap on the closet doorknob, a Nikon camera complete with zoom lens seemed to stare at us; and three boxes of Polaroid film lay scattered on the floor near the bed. I remembered Andrea.

"You're so sexy, let me tell you a dream," I said, my lips grazing his ear. "Last night I was at a party with some girls who model for *Penthouse*—a dozen brazen centerfolds." His breathing grew deeper. "The only man in the room was a photographer who didn't seem attracted to women, so I called and invited you to join us, insisting you bring along your camera."

"Oh, you *know* me!" he exclaimed, shocked. Then a puzzled expression crept across his face, as if he were trying to decide whether to play along or not. He cupped my face in his hands and stared at me.

"I'm in big trouble," he whispered, smiling sweetly, covering my face with tiny kisses. "You've hooked me, you know."

I winked at him. "Let me finish. I haven't gotten to the good part . . ." And smiling wickedly, I continued to weave my verbal web of seduction that climaxed in an extraordinary night of physical passion. That was three years ago.

Today we are still passionate lovers, growing daily with each other's needs and desires, delighting in an accepting, loving, adult relationship.

When, after a few months of sexual bliss, I asked when he first realized that we would fall so deeply in love, he answered, "That very first time, when you whispered in my ear."

WHISPER IN HIS EAR

LESSON 1

Whispering in His Ear or The Art of Aural Sex

Only ten years ago sexologists wrote reams of research papers which tried to make oral sex respectable. Now in the 1980's, as we bask in tingling sensations after putting our fingers on our "G-spots," chat with friends over lunch about multiple orgasms, and trot into Saks Fifth Avenue for lacy garterbelts, we are approaching an era of total sexual openness. Wanting to reward both ourselves and our sexual partners, we find ourselves needing to go beyond sheer sexual intercourse to a more complete experience that satisfies more than our bodies. The time has come to orchestrate all our senses together. We all know men get excited simply seeing a naked woman, but what about *hearing* one? As you excite each other's senses with visual and spoken clues, love and passion burn brightly.

Are you ready to graduate from "I love you" to "make love to me," from "make love to me" to "fuck me hard and deep"? If so, this book will provide the lessons you need to improve your lovemaking with *aural* sex.

Are You Ready for Erotic Stories?

Aural sex forges one ultimate link in the lover's chain. The sounds of sex can range from simple cries of pleasure to long, cleverly spun fantasy-stories. When should you employ aural sex? That depends.

Sexual therapists prescribe explicit conversation to help people share their true sexual feelings with one another, but a word of caution: if you or your partner suffer a physical or psychological disability, you should seek professional counseling or therapy because no book, not even this one, can replace the skill and guidance you may need. On the other hand, fantasy stories *do work,* provided you and your man are free from serious physical or psychological problems that require medical attention. So be sensitive to your unique situation and if appropriate, put off telling fantasy-stories until a more suitable time.

Many couples should wait until they've firmly established a loving, trusting adult relationship, while others can immediately convert a casual date into an unforgettable evening with a fantasy story. In any case, it won't hurt to take your time, gradually perfecting your technique and subtly finding the keys to your man's secret fantasy life by completing his Sexual Fantasy Inventory. Still, if you are quick-witted and confident you could, with a little bit of luck, pull one off the first time you make love, as I did with Ryan. I don't recommend you tell your lover a fantasy story every time you make love, because you should always strive to retain the thrill of hot, loving sex. I weave most of my own fantasy stories at special times—anniversaries, birthdays, celebrating a raise—and for those times when I want a little extra steam in my love life. Always try to change each fantasy story a little, even after you've struck the magic chord that has him ready to batter down doors for you.

Even if you're familiar with your man's sexual turn-ons, you've probably only seen the tip of the iceberg because most men shy away from admitting anyone into their innermost fantasy world, and many are themselves unaware of their own deepest secrets which may lie buried under layers of shame and guilt.

Noelle and Sam Prentiss, an attractive couple in their late thirties, have been married for twelve years. Sam Prentiss is a dynamic, highly successful theatrical lawyer with many beautiful women among his clients. Not once during their courtship and marriage has either Sam or Noelle been unfaithful. "Noelle turns me on like no woman can," boasts Sam. What does Noelle do? Quite simply, once every few weeks Noelle tailors a fantasy story to her husband's desires. Here's one that drives Sam wild:

"The other night I dreamed I was a judge and you were a lawyer trying a case in my court. While you were questioning a female witness whose large, firm breasts stretched her knit pullover to bursting, I noticed a bulge in your pants. Were you getting an erection? The thought made me so excited that I couldn't stand it any longer and ordered a short recess, demanding that you join me in my chambers

for a conference. Once I got you behind closed doors I sat on the edge of my desk and let my robes fall aside to reveal a pair of pink crotchless panties. I started to caress myself and lick my lips. You blushed, but I ordered you to play with me or I'd hold you in contempt. When you slid your finger inside me I moaned and begged you to take me. I discarded my robe and began playing with my breasts until my nipples were hard as raisins. You got so excited you pulled my panties off and made love to me right there on my desk. We really did each other justice."

Sam Prentiss, like many other men, often slips into a fantasy world to reach the pinnacle of erotic pleasure during lovemaking. Bookstores and magazine racks overflow with material devoted to satisfying such appetites. While a man loves to find himself in bed with a woman who is open and excited by her own sexuality, that same man will go stark, raving wild if his lover learns to tell him his *own* fantasies. So here it is—a collection of stories men wish their lovers would tell them during lovemaking, and all the tools you need to create your own unique ones.

Adding the Romantic Touches

The bookracks in supermarkets testify to the fact that women crave romance. Whether your man admits to it or not, he craves it, too. Sex without romance is like salad without dressing—it may fill you up, but it's flat and unsatisfying.

When you create your fantasy stories be sure to add romantic touches—filmy negligées, sexy underwear, erotic settings, exciting music. Not only will these touches turn him on, they will help stimulate *you.*

Even the most macho man wants more than just

dirty talk. My friend Justin opened my eyes to this early in my research when he told me:

"Modern women are more open about what they want in bed. I've dated and slept with fifty or sixty women, many of whom have directed my lovemaking from beginning to end. They issue orders like a drill sergeant—'Take me now,' or worse, 'Now I'm gonna make you come.' I feel like a piece of meat, wondering where good, old-fashioned romance has gone. If a woman takes the time and effort to find out my favorite color, clothes style, and environment, she's telling me she cares about me."

When you create your fantasy stories, remember Justin's advice. He may be a bit jaded, but most men have seen so many stark naked women playing with themselves in men's magazines that they find moonlight shining through your sheer nightgown a refreshingly erotic sight.

The Brain: The Most Powerful Sexual Organ

"Sure I get an erection when she touches my penis, but I have to crawl deep inside my brain to come."

The ears are the portals to the mind. Although a man's erection may depend on physiological and psychological stimulation, his brain controls orgasm. To reach an orgasm, men must give themselves permission, permission derived from all their sexual experiences since childhood. Therefore, to really control your man sexually, you must understand *what turned the little boy you never knew into the man you love*.

How to Release the Little Boy in Your Man

When your man brushes against your ear, creating a tingle with his warm breath, and whispers "Later, baby," he has already begun to make love to you. And when you pluck the cherry from his ice cream sundae and nibble at it seductively while he watches, you are having visual intercourse with him.

Just think of these little hints as the foreplay to aural sex. The way you tease your man before you reveal his fantasy story can have him chomping at the bit, bucking and begging for more. Just as a partially clothed woman is often sexier to a man than a totally naked one, a gentle thrill before telling a powerful fantasy story can improve the results of your seduction.

You have his mother to thank for this phenomenon; bedtime stories gave your man his earliest thrills. When your man was a little boy he was often coaxed into his bed with the promise of a story. He learned to toddle off to bed eager for his reward: a trip to the land of make-believe. Would the prince slay the dragon and rescue the damsel? Would Lassie survive the black river and find her way home?

With the techniques you learn from this book, you will be able to replace childish bedtime stories with adult ones. Don't be surprised if later on you feel a gentle tugging at your sleeve from your "Wizard of Wall Street" and he whispers in *your* ear—"Tell me a story in bed tonight, honey."

I've never met a man who didn't like to be asked what he was like as a little boy. Ask to see your man's high school yearbook, or better yet, a picture of his Cub Scout troop or Little League baseball team. And I'll bet that if you pry a little, your man will be delighted to tell you about his first sexual experience.

A Harvard professor I interviewed gleefully told me about Mildred, the choir director in his church who seduced him when he was fourteen. When she got him into bed, she urged him to make believe he was taking a shower and rubbing soap over his penis. As she made love to him she spurred him on by saying, "Remember how nice that hot slippery soap felt on your pee-pee?" Then Mildred performed oral sex on him. Did he feel guilt? Not for a minute, since Mildred convinced him that somewhere in the Bible it said that a woman shall suckle a young babe at her breast. After relating his story, this world-renowned professor giggled boyishly, beamed at me, and confided, "She called me *young babe*!" When I asked if his wife knew the story, he cried, "No!" But when I asked what would happen if she started calling him "young babe" while they were making love, he wiggled in his seat and blushed deeply. Huskily he confessed, "I'd love it."

Since men were youngsters, reading comic books or hot rod magazines, they dreamed of being in certain sexual situations.

Observe teenaged Rodney who lies in bed drooling over a picture of a fire-engine-red Corvette with a gorgeous girl draped across the hood. As he looks at the picture he strokes his penis. He'd love to take that girl to a secluded spot in his Corvette and have sex with her on the hood.

Even in adulthood, just the *thought* of doing something with someone, the *thought* of having someone do something to him, or the *thought* of watching someone do something to themselves will charge a man's sexual drive. So it makes sense that you can turn your man on simply by planting, at the right moment, the right thoughts in his head. Most young boys are strongly influenced by mothers who discouraged stray little hands from genitals, saying, "Don't do that or you'll grow warts," followed by young girls who insisted that boys' "things" were dirty, and finally by teenaged girls who drove them to the point of ecstasy, only to remove groping hands with the stern admonishment,

"Nice girls don't do that!" Having encountered so many "no" women, a man will certainly fantasize about the "yes" woman he's always yearned to meet.

The Difference Between Fantasies and Fantasy Stories

Fantasies are what we secretly wish would happen to us or someone else; fantasy stories, on the other hand, are "faction"—fantasies with facts cleverly woven into a story suited to a particular lover. Once you have mastered the art of customizing fantasy stories for a lover, no other woman will be able to feed him your special brand of erotic excitement. Only *you* will be able to exploit the unique memories, wishes, and experiences that trigger his passion.

Overcoming Stage Fright

The stories that capture the male imagination seldom bear a close resemblance to the reality of everyday life. A short, fat accountant may fantasize that he is a slim tennis pro with a clientele of lithe young debutantes all hot for his body. If you feel uncomfortable relating fantasy stories to your man, relax. Remember, you'll be telling him a story, just like reading to him from a juicy novel. As a matter of fact, in the beginning you will tell him someone *else's* fantasies, albeit fantasies guaranteed to get a rise out of almost any man.

Sherry, a plain, slightly overweight schoolteacher coupled two fairly common fantasies her man confided to her (being a sports hero and watching her have sex with another man) into an uncommon story. It concludes with her lover batting with two outs in the bottom of the ninth inning in the tied seventh game of the World Series while she's sitting in the stands with her hands in another guy's pants.

Unleashing Your Own Powerful Sex Drive

Because most men harbor strong preconceived notions regarding a woman's sex drive (remember the teenaged girls in the back seats who never went "all the way"?) many men underestimate a woman's erotic power. Don't confuse this with the madonna-and-whore syndrome, where men marry "nice girls" and have sex with "bad girls." It's not that simple. For generations, men have been programmed to think of themselves as the more erotic sex, a myth reinforced by the fact that until the past few years, 98% of all erotica was designed for a strictly male audience.

Men who would gleefully share a dirty joke with co-workers, grab at each other's genitals in the locker room, and brag about sexual conquests in the car on the way to work, were shocked when they discovered that all along women had been *thinking* about precisely what men had been *talking* about. When Erica Jong wrote *Fear of Flying*, more than one reviewer exclaimed, "Wow, she thinks and writes like a man!" Today, more and more women are comparing notes on oral sex, sharing special bedroom techniques, and openly admiring a big bulge in a pair of jeans or a well-shaped rear.

Fantasy Stories and the Liberated Woman

In this age of complete honesty, of equally shared experiences and of letting it all hang out, women could argue with themselves against resorting to fantasies to heighten a sexual relationship. And some sexual therapists may holler like hell that it's healthier to learn to get off without any props or fantasies, that only the purity of the moment counts. Oh, I don't disagree. Rather, I would add that yes, while all that's true, the really sophisticated woman knows that shaking a little spice over well-seasoned minds can result in undreamed of gourmet delights.

After conceiving of the idea for this book, I was concerned how my feminist friends in Cambridge would respond to it. A trip to a hockey game with one of my closest friends opened my eyes.

One cold, wintry morning my friend Adrienne picked up my son and me for a trip to a hockey tournament. Her live-in lover, Nathaniel, sat in the front seat next to her while her son rode in back with us. Adrienne has a Ph.D. in modern languages, teaches at a major university, and always speaks out for women's rights: "I hate the games women have to play to soothe and captivate their men, Liane." As I shivered in the back seat nursing a hot cup of coffee, I observed Adrienne talking with Nathaniel. Her normally clear, authoritative voice had changed to a simpering little girl's as she asked him where he'd like to have lunch. "At a restaurant, or home in front of a fire?" she purred. Nathaniel, a computer scientist at M.I.T., lisped back, "At home, Mommy." "If you're a good boy, Mommy will tell you a story," Adrienne cooed.

Well, I was shocked by the babytalk, but I tucked away the information, telling myself that the next time she launched into one of her liberation speeches, I'd remind her how she holds *her* man.

EXERCISE 1

Popular Fantasies

You'll need:

A selection of men's magazines such as *Penthouse, Playboy,* or *Forum*
Felt-tip pen
Peace and quiet

Almost all newsstands and convenience stores stock magazines that cater to men's erotic fantasies. Read some from cover to cover, paying attention not only to the models, but also to the advertisements for such products as cars and stereos which have been designed to fulfill a man's secret wishes. Mark those that impress you. In my opinion, *Penthouse* and *Forum* skillfully incorporate the most universally appealing fantasies, and you'll undoubtedly find one or two that will turn you or your man on.

Choose three or four of the readers' letters you find most interesting, study them, and read them aloud to yourself. Notice the characters, the setting, the action, the language.

LESSON 2

Acting School

Donna Marshall, a beautiful divorcée in her early forties, flitted from bed to bed in a series of unsatisfying one-night stands, but she yearned for a more meaningful relationship with a man. When she met a handsome, successful film producer, she decided to bait a trap. During a stroll along the beach and over a romantic seaside dinner, she played to his ego by asking penetrating questions about his childhood and adolescence. Soon she learned he'd been bullied in school by an All-American quarterback named Gregory, who eventually married a nurse. After watching a couple of the producer's films, she concluded that he liked to see women touching each other. Armed with these few facts, Donna spun the following fantasy story for her target which prompted a marriage proposal!

"While I was driving my silver Porsche home I daydreamed that you were visiting your doctor for your yearly checkup. After giving you a clean bill of health your doctor told you to get dressed while he examined another patient. Just as you stepped into your shorts, two chattering nurses walked into the room, recoiled when they saw you half-naked, then apologized. Blushing yourself, you nevertheless thought you recognized the taller of the two women, a long-legged redhead with mischievous green eyes. When she smiled, you realized it was Gregory's wife. With one hand, she reached behind her back to lock the door, while with the other she undid the top button of her white dress, revealing her freckled chest. When your penis twitched she ran the tip of her tongue across her lips. Her hard nipples strained through her uniform. 'How about giving me a little injection?' she teased. The other nurse, a short, plump blonde with lush breasts and a round ass, giggled and quickly slipped her uniform over her head.

While Gregory's wife stroked your chest and pulled down your shorts, the blonde stripped her, too. Gregory's wife had small, high tits and her pubic hair blazed bright red, as if her core were on fire. 'Eat me,' she urged the blonde, who quickly knelt to obey. You positioned yourself so Gregory's wife could softly stroke your manhood. 'I want to be the first to suck you off,' she said. But when the blonde squeezed her breasts around your penis, you couldn't hold back and ejaculated all over her chest. You watched Gregory's wife lick the come off the other woman's breasts, then you had sex with her while she ate her friend. 'Your cock is twice as big as Gregory's,' she confided after her third orgasm."

Homework the Teacher Never Assigned

Remember, research provides the key to unlocking your man's special fantasy world. Any woman can talk dirty to a man, punctuating lovemaking with four-letter words, but you can maximize your man's sexual response, as you can your own, by adding romantic touches and playing to his hidden fears and desires. Some of the most erotic fantasies omit dirty words and graphic sex in favor of moonlit beaches and wet T-shirts. Comedienne Joan Rivers jokes that her husband is so British that when he gets off he calmly says, "I have *arrived.*"

A woman may feel she knows her man intimately simply because they have shared the same bed, but she may forget that much of any man's fantasy life began long before she arrived on the scene. You can live intimately with one man for twenty years without discovering the types of erotica he finds most exciting.

How will you know what your man likes? Only by doing your homework. This involves careful planning, asking the right questions at the right times, and paying strict attention to details you may have formerly overlooked.

The Other Woman

Another woman? Absolutely. Because so many sexually stimulating fantasy stories involve other women, other men, and groups, you must replace any jealousy with curiosity and come to terms with past or imaginary other women now. Why not feel grateful to the first few girls who let your man practice with them, only to let him drift away into your arms later? If you feel hopelessly jealous, then fantasize about the other woman without her makeup on, in a dowdy housedress, or going to the bathroom. If your man's "other woman" is young and svelte, picture her as fat, bitchy, and old. Does she threaten you, do you fear you'll be planting seeds of infidelity in your man's head? Don't be silly. Regardless of the beauty or sexual prowess of your fictional rival, *you* will retain control of your lover's fantasies. If the goal of your fantasizing is a superb sex session, you, not Marilyn (Monroe, Chambers, or the girl next door) will be on the receiving end of the spine-shattering climax. Why not let your man pretend he's writhing in a harem while in reality he's safely tucked into your warm bed? While his brain frolics on a nude beach on the Riviera with three uninhibited Swedish starlets, the rest of him will be wrapped firmly and lovingly in your unique and familiar embrace.

Men Love Women Who Ask Questions

Curiosity may have killed a few cats, but it's essential if you're going to find your way through the labyrinths of your man's psyche, scrutinizing every single clue, searching for the subliminal fascination which most men keep well hidden.

For example, one man I interviewed confessed that he longed to watch two women make love to each other while he photographed them. "Oh, I just want to watch, not screw," he insisted. Had I been a novice interviewer, I might have accepted his insistence. But I persisted, inviting him to flesh out his fantasy until two and a half hours later I had discovered the truth. True, he did not wish to screw the cuddling women, he wanted *them* to tie *him* up, then screw him. How did I do it? When I asked him to tell me about the sexiest photograph he'd ever seen, he described a shot from a men's magazine in which two female German officers capture an American pilot and torture him with sex.

A picture's worth a thousand words, so try to get your man to describe photos or films that turn him on, then figure out why he responds to them. Better yet, have him show you such pictures, and take copious mental notes. How many people are in them? What kind of people? What are they wearing and how have they fixed their hair? Are their stockings fishnet or silk? At the end of this chapter I'll show you how to turn this task into an exciting sexual encounter.

Learning How to Be an Investigative Reporter

What do investigative reporters have in common? Most begin by doggedly pursuing a tip or a hunch. Gradually they start to gather bits and pieces of information without letting their targets suspect their intentions. Then they fit the pieces together to determine missing information needed to flesh out the story. To uncover *your* man's story, you must take care never to tip your hand. Stimulate your man to supply initial clues by asking the sorts of innocent questions that flatter men's egos:

- You must have had a lot of girls chasing you in high school. Did you date a lot of them?
- I bet your first lover still dreams about you. What was she like?
- Did your mother ever allow you to see her naked? How did you feel about that?
- Your work sounds fascinating. Do you meet a lot of interesting women? Do you ever make love to them?
- Did anyone ever tell you you have the most marvelous bedroom eyes?

Don't confide that you plan to eventually weave fantasy stories for him. If you blow your cover you could sacrifice the stunning thrill of opening night.

Clues

A woman medical student said she'd determined her man got excited whenever she wore new silk underwear and she had thought she'd even narrowed it down to style, color, and manufacturer. But when an expensive, new red silk bra and matching panties had no effect the third time she wore them, she finally discovered that it was the new clothes' *smell* that delighted him. When he'd said, "I love to rub my nose against your *new* panties," she had failed to pick up on a seemingly insignificant comment.

Pay attention to details. Does his roving eye settle on shapely legs, large breasts, or valentine asses? Does the color purple or a slinky black dress turn him on? What theme dominates the off-color jokes he tells his friends?

To make sure you consider as many details as possible, you can complete your man's Sexual Fantasy Inventory.

Just answer the questions on the next few pages. If you can supply several answers to one question, you'll unearth clues for your treasury of fantasy stories. Be thoughtful and thorough.

Slip into something comfortable, turn on the stereo, take out your pen, and begin to create:

Your Man's Sexual Fantasy Inventory

General Background Information

1. What kind of a car did he drive as a kid?

2. What kind of car did he wish he drove?
3. What is his dream car? Write down color, interior, and extras.

Hobbies

1. What does he do to relax?
2. Does he have a regular hobby?

HINT: Browse through a large toy and sporting goods store with him to see what catches his eye.

On the Job

1. Does he love his work?
2. If not, what does he wish he did for a living?
3. Whom at the office does he most admire?
4. Who, in his office, turns him on?
5. Has he ever thought about having sex at the office? If so, with whom?

HINT: Meet him for lunch at his office some day and mention the cute little redhead who works with him. Watch his response carefully.

Possessions

1. What does he have that he cherishes?
2. What do *you* have that he wants?
3. What would he like to give you? Jewels, furs, cars?
4. What would he like you to give him? A Betamax, paintings, or a nude photo of yourself?

HINT: Try to spend a little time alone in his home to leisurely examine his reading matter, and any collections he may have of paintings or photographs. Next time the winning lottery number is announced ask him how he would spend the winnings. You'll learn a great deal about the inner man.

Entertainment

1. How would he describe his "perfect evening"?
2. Whom would he spend it with?
3. Where would it take place?
4. What kinds of books or movies does he enjoy?
5. Has he ever yearned to be a writer or director?
6. What would be the plot of his masterpiece?
7. What does he like to do on a rainy day?

HINT: Tell him about a great book you just finished reading or discuss one you've both read. If he could write a book or make a movie, what would it be about?

Food

1. What are his favorite foods?
2. Does he believe some foods are aphrodisiacs?

Living Quarters

1. What kind of home does he live in?
2. How is his favorite room decorated?
3. Describe his fantasy dream house.

HINT: Thumb through a magazine like *Better Homes and Gardens* or *Architectural Digest*. When he sees a house he likes, ask him what kind of furniture he would buy. Would he install a hot tub or sauna?

Vacations

1. What is his favorite spot in the world?
2. Where does he dream of going?
3. Whom does he dream of going with?
4. What would he like to do when he gets there?

HINT: Visit a travel agent and collect a variety of brochures which you can leave lying around. Be adventuresome, clip the specialty ads from the *New*

Yorker for trekking in the Himalayas. Review them with him.

Color

1. What is his favorite color for himself? For women? (Consider clothes, underwear, hair, complexion, car, and bed sheets.)
2. Does he dislike a certain color?

HINT: Stroll into a designer dress shop and ask him to point out the dresses he likes. Notice the color, style, and fabric. Encourage him to choose something *he* likes, rather than an item that he thinks you would choose for yourself.

His Youth

1. Did he masturbate as a child? Alone or with someone else? Was he afraid of getting caught?
2. With whom did he have his first sexual experience (not necessarily intercourse)?
3. Who spurned him in high school?
4. Who was his teenage dream girl (girlfriend, actress)?
5. Who was his favorite teacher?
6. Who was his favorite coach?
7. Who bullied him when he was a kid?
8. What sports did he play?
9. What sports did he wish he had played?

HINT: Ask him to show you his old yearbook or tell you stories about his fondest, scariest, or most exciting memories.

Women

1. Who is his fantasy woman?
2. Is she passive or aggressive?

3. Is she talkative or quiet?
4. Is she vivacious or shy?
5. Is she younger or older than he?
6. Is she bitchy or babyish?
7. How does she smell? Perfumed, fresh, or gamey?
8. Does she shave her underarms, her legs?
9. Would he like to have sex with women from races other than from his own?
10. Would he like to have sex with athletes or entertainers? A girls' soccer team?

HINT: Collect an array of fashion magazines such as *Cosmopolitan* or even the front section of the *New York Times*. Tell him you are running an imaginary beauty contest to create the perfect woman. Have him leaf through the photos pointing out perfect toes, nose, tits, and ass.

Who's in Control?

1. In his fantasy is he aggressive or passive?
2. Would he like to be a slave to his queen?
3. Who reaches orgasm first? Or is it simultaneous?
4. Who is on top?
5. What's his favorite position?
6. What position does he long to try?

HINT: View an erotic film with him and ask him about the action in the film with different sexual positions.

Audio

1. What is his favorite type of music for dancing?
2. Does he enjoy making love to music?
3. Who are his favorite male and female vocalists?
4. Does he like you to make sounds while making love?

5. Does he like to make sounds while making love?
6. Is he intrigued by spoken accents? Foreign, southern, or preppy?

Pornography

1. Does he read pornography? Note: He may hide it.
2. What pictures in porno books turn him on the most?
3. Would he like to photograph models for pornographic magazines?
4. Would he like *you* to model for a porno magazine or movie?
5. Has he made a porno phonecall to a professional service?

Language

1. What does he call his penis?
2. What does he call your vagina?
3. What does he call sexual intercourse?
4. What does he call oral sex performed on him?
5. What does he call oral sex performed on women?
6. What does he call ejaculation?
7. What does he call anal sex?

HINT: Listen to him tell a joke to another man at a cocktail party, or ask him to tell you his favorite ones, keeping in mind he may not use his most graphic language with you. Pay close attention to the swear words he uses, such as when his favorite team makes a disastrous mistake in an important game.

Visuals

1. Does he like to watch while you make love to him?
2. Does he want you to watch while making love?
3. Does he want to be watched by others?

HINT: Ask what he would do if the neighbors walked in while you were in a clinch. Then test his reaction, and don't be fooled. If you say, "Harold, if the neighbors popped in on us, would you stop or continue?" and Harold insists he'd stop but you notice he's getting an erection, he's lying.

Props

1. Would he like to see you in a costume?
2. Would he like to wear a costume? Your underwear, for example?
3. Would he like to use a vibrator on you?
4. Would he like you to use a vibrator on him?
5. Would he like to see you use a dildo?
6. Would he like you to use a dildo on him?

HINT: Buy an inexpensive sex toy, gift wrap it, and give it to him as a joke. After you both laugh about it, you may be surprised to find a serious use for it.

His Erotic Zones

1. Other than his genitals, where is he most sensitive? Does he respond to caresses on his chest, neck, nipples, eyelashes, ears, hair, waist, belly, small of back, arms, fingers, toes, arches, ankles, inside of calves, inside of knees, inside of thighs, buttocks, anus, scrotum, shaft of penis, rim of penis, tip of penis, or pubic hair?
2. Compare these erotic zones with your own, looking for interesting match-ups such as tickling his balls with your nipples, a dual turn-on.

Fleshing Out the Story

Study this example of how you might brew a fantasy story out of a few clues.

The Other Woman

After watching an old "beach blanket bingo" movie on TV with your man, you ask him about his date for the senior prom. Though he'd taken his steady girl, he had always admired the beautiful black-haired flirt who had been elected prom queen. Her looks and bold sexuality had always intimidated him, but he had secretly wished he were the one by her side the night of the prom.

Audio

He likes music from the fifties, and his favorite song is "Earth Angel." (Have it playing in the background the night you tell your first fantasy story, or hand him a custom-made cassette of his favorite music with instructions to play it when he drives to pick you up for the crucial date.)

Visual

He subscribes to *Playboy* but does not like more explicit magazines such as *Penthouse* or *Hustler.* (Since you know *Playboy* caters to younger college-age men, this provides another valuable clue.)

Heroes

Among his heroes is Robert Kennedy, whose boyish good looks and idealistic politics he greatly admired.

Possessions

He drives a Datsun 280 ZX, which he calls "the poor man's Porsche." Naturally, it is his favorite color, bronze. He water-skis every chance he gets and would love to own an expensive speedboat.

Leisure Time

If he could vacation anywhere in the world, he would pick a mountain lake where he could water-ski. Of course, he says he'd want you there in order to make it perfect.

With only these six categories of information at hand you could embroider a fairly elaborate script. And don't forget that men enjoy romance and foreplay as much as women, so put some effort into the setting. Let's say you've invited him to your place for dinner. After you eat, you snuggle up on the couch with snifters of warm brandy and begin to whisper in his ear:

"I had a sexy dream last night. I'm almost embarrassed to tell you about it, but you were the star! *In the dream, I was a little taller, with jet-black hair, and was working in your campaign for the U.S. Senate. You reminded me so much of Bobby Kennedy. One night we stayed late at the campaign headquarters (I was just an anonymous staff worker, but I could tell you liked me because you kept staring at my long legs). When you invited me to take a spin on your new speedboat, I instantly accepted, and we were soon zooming across a beautiful mountain lake in the moonlight. You told me that you loved my dress, the same one I'm wearing now. While you drove the boat with one hand, you put the other around my shoulders. To your delight, you could feel my bare breasts beneath my dress, but you were in for an even bigger surprise, because I had slipped off my panties and had tossed them into the boat's wake. Since my pussy was getting really wet, I asked you to stop the boat so I could take a swim. I hadn't brought my bikini and so I proposed that we skinny-dip. Swiftly, I pulled my dress over my head. My nipples were hard as pebbles, and I*

squeezed them between my fingers while imagining sticking them in your mouth. But I turned and dove into the water, swimming around the boat, sometimes diving so you could admire my ass, sometimes floating on my back. Later we made love with the waves gently rocking the boat."

Let's examine this script. Obviously it exploits the prom-queen and political-idol dreams, but it also displays a few subtleties. First of all, like the pictures and stories in *Playboy,* the woman's body and the sex are not described very graphically. The woman focuses on *her* body, not the man's, and she plays a relatively subdued temptress. If the man admired *Penthouse* and longed to have sex with a Hollywood sex star, the story might contain more explicit language.

Using the Inventory to Create a Story

Marsha, a sophisticated black marketing executive, had lived with Ken, a physician, for three years. They were very compatible, both sexually and as friends. But as happy as they were, Ken had a roving eye and several times each year would slip away for a sexual encounter with a woman not nearly as attractive as Marsha. When he confessed his infidelities, he simply said, "They're dirtier." After struggling with her jealousy for some time, Marsha finally decided to try to act a little dirtier herself. Her first fantasy-story illustrates how to be a subtle, yet thorough, investigative reporter. I've taken the liberty of putting the clues of Ken's fantasies in italics.

One afternoon, as they were sitting in a hot tub, Marsha asked, "Who's the biggest ladies' man at the hospital?"

"Chuck," Ken answered. "A lot of the women residents chase him, and he told me that he can make any woman *come three or four times* before he even puts his cock in. He is into kinky stuff, too."

"You mean whips and chains?" Marsha probed.

"Black satin garter belts and silk stockings. He's got pictures of women taped inside his locker. They're touching each other's *cunts*."

"Cunts?" Ken had always referred to Marsha's vagina as a pussy. Marsha tucked away the clue.

Later that week, as they watched the Superbowl, Marsha asked, "You were a good athlete in high school, weren't you, Ken?"

"Yes, but not good enough to *turn pro* like these guys."

"Would you have liked that?" she asked.

"Well maybe for a couple of years it would have been fun." Marsha watched very carefully as Ken turned his attention back to the game, then she filed away another important clue.

With this newfound knowledge, Marsha completed Ken's sexual fantasy inventory. From living with him she knew that he loved to come in her mouth, had been very turned on by the feel of her silk underwear, frequently read *Penthouse* and, occasionally, *Hustler*, liked aggressive women, and referred to his penis as a cock.

Marsha incorporated this information into the following script:

"While watching a football game the other day I pretended you were the quarterback. You won the game with a spectacular 80-yard pass in the final seconds. After the game I invited you to a private celebration at my place. When you got there I opened the door wearing nothing but a black garter belt and silk stockings. You got so hard the minute you saw me that it was only minutes before I had your cock in my mouth. . . ."

As she became more comfortable with the idea of creating a fantasy, she created a more elaborate fantasy story:

"Let's make believe that you were the star quarterback in this year's Superbowl and that your team won the game on your last-second 80-yard touchdown pass. I loved you so much and was so proud of you, I couldn't wait to put my arms around you.

"After the game we went back to the hotel for a private celebration. Room service delivered champagne and pheasant which we ate by candlelight. After dinner I told you I had a surprise, and I slowly stripped off the peasant dress I had worn to the game to reveal that I was wearing nothing but a white garter belt and silk stockings with seams running up the backs of my legs. My breasts and ass were free for you to admire, and you told me I looked especially beautiful this night. I said my cunt had become very wet watching you play the game and that throughout the last quarter I had been thinking about sucking you. When I noticed the swelling underneath the fabric of your trousers, I carefully removed your clothes, admiring your hard, muscular body. Then I fished a pair of white satin panties out of my bag and asked you to slip them on. You loved the feeling of the soft silk against your hard cock. Suddenly, I felt my heart skip a beat as you ran your fingers along the inside of my thighs. You felt my wetness. Without removing your panties, you started rubbing your cock against my cunt, relishing the heat. You soon removed your cock from the constraint of the panties and slid it down my throat.

"Soon I asked you to lie down on the couch so I could straddle your head and rub my cunt over your lips. The candles flickered, Streisand sang us love songs and, as you licked me and tasted the perfume of

my loins, I reached behind myself and slid a finger into your asshole. You begged me not to stop.

"When we finally began to fuck, you frantically thrust your cock into me until I came in screaming bursts of pleasure. You felt me tighten and release, over and over and over; you knew that you pleased me more than any man could please any woman.

"Finally, when I thought I might die from our love-making, I whispered in your ear that I wanted you to come in my mouth. And then I swallowed your cock deep into my throat. The thought excited you so much, you couldn't hold back. Your sweet burning come flooded my mouth and I swallowed most of it, but saved a little to dip on my fingers and rub onto your hardened nipples. Then I sighed that you were the best lover in the world. Because you really are!"

EXERCISE 2

Creating Your First Fantasy Script

You'll need:

Several explicit men's magazines (*Playboy, Penthouse, Hustler, Chic, Club, Cheri*—any book with quality color pictures and advertisements will do).
1 sexy outfit or negligee
1 pair of scissors
1 roll of transparent tape
2 felt-tip pens, one red, one blue
1 8½" × 11" spiral notebook or three-ring binder

To begin:

If you don't already know, find out if your target lover ever reads men's magazines.

HINT: Tell him someone recommended to you a fantastic article in *Penthouse* on defense spending (or whatever else you know interests your man), that you read it, and that you not only found it well-done but you were also fascinated by the *Forum* letters and by a photograph of a stunning model.

Setting the trap:

Take him home or go to his place. Either buy the magazines yourself or count on him having them available. Tell him you'd like to share a magazine with him. Begin turning pages together. Observe his expression while looking at the pictures. (A secret smile tells all, and a hand on your shoulder might even set the stage for a pleasant interruption.) Since men love to be asked questions about themselves, quiz him about what he sees (stereos, cars, clothes, booze, models). This will help you complete his inventory. Finally, draw out his comments about the sexy articles or the pictures.

Springing the trap:

Urge him to choose his favorite photograph. Cut it out and tape it on a page in the notebook you have handy. Ask him to write a funny caption, or write one yourself. You can turn this into a game, alternating photos with a little dialogue until you've filled about a dozen pages. Not only will you have a permanent record of his fantasies, but you can reveal *your* fantasies to your man this way, too.

It's not fattening, but it is sinful!

LESSON 3

Tryouts

Nicholas Weatherbee—heir to an oil fortune, educated at Harvard and the London School of Economics, connoisseur of beautiful women, sleek, expensive race horses, and fine art—spent a couple hours with me one cold, snowy night in the Ritz Carlton's bar. I had been interviewing him for an article on eligible young bachelors. But as so often happens, the conversation eventually drifted to sex.

After a couple Beefeater martinis (stirred, not shaken), he loosened up and began to reveal his own favorite fantasy story, told to him by Jessica, a cool southern belle he had always assumed to be the personification of propriety. But Jessica had set her cap for Weatherbee and had cagily concocted this fantasy-story in order to capture him.

"Darling, I imagined sitting at the bar in Gilley's (a notorious country and western roadhouse near Houston whose mechanical bull John Travolta rode in the movie Urban Cowboy*), wearing a red satin cowgirl blouse, skintight jeans and handtooled snakeskin boots with shiny silver spurs. I had my black hair teased up high and sprinkled with little rhinestone flowers.*

"It was a hot, humid night. When several big men crowded close to watch a friend ride the bull, I spun my stool around and casually unbuttoned my shirt until everyone could see the white tops of my breasts. One man even held a frosty beer against them, suggesting we go outside to cool off. But just then you walked into the bar wearing tight jeans that clearly outlined your manhood. Did you catch me staring at it? Is that why you picked me out of that roomful of hot, horny women?

"When you managed to shoulder your way through the crowd to the stool next to me I got a whiff of your musk cologne mingled with the smell of horses. Soon you asked me to dance to a slow Willie Nelson song. And when we got out on the dance floor I started rubbing my breasts against you so hard that you stood at attention in a minute. Did it surprise you when I cupped your ass in my hand?

"When the song ended I whispered 'Honey, let's go out to my van.' You quickly agreed, provided that I first rode the mechanical bull. All the men clapped when I climbed aboard, grasping the reins in one hand, flicking free another button on my blouse with the other. Mercifully, someone put the bull on its slowest speed, so I managed to hold on despite the sweet sweat slicking my chest and thighs. Each time

the bull bucked, I could feel my breasts bouncing further and further out of my blouse, and my pussy felt like it had been banged for an hour.

"After I finally scrambled down, everyone applauded, but I ran straight to your side, my left breast fully exposed, and insisted you come outside to cool me down. Once inside my van, I ordered you to close your eyes while I changed shirts. My red satin one was so wet and sticky. Were you shocked when you opened your eyes to see me lying stark naked on the custom waterbed in the back of my van? 'This is how I cool down,' I laughed, running my hands from my wet thighs to my slick breasts. 'All you have to do is blow on me. But don't touch!' I purred. I could tell it drove you crazy leaning over my naked body and gently blowing until I was almost dry. Then I smiled wickedly. 'My turn,' I said. 'But I do *get to touch.'*

"Soon I stripped you naked and began kissing and licking your body until your dick quivered. Rolling my tongue around your dick's lovely tulip-shaped head, I slowly sucked its full length down my throat and pumped hard until you came. You didn't think a nice girl like me would swallow it all, did you?"

For Nicholas Weatherbee, Jessica's fantasy-story fit squarely into a secret world he never even realized had existed. Sure, he'd fantasized about pristine virgins who would shuck their shyness and abandon their virtue at the sight of his manhood, but he had never found one. He had concluded that such women didn't really exist. As he had confessed to me that snowy night, Jessica was the first "yes" woman he had ever met. And they had gone on to actually *do* all the things she fabricated in her stories.

"She says she's not ready for marriage," sighed Nicholas. "But she's the only woman I'll ever need." I saw the pleasure in his eyes when Jessica strolled into the bar to join us. In her beige cashmere sweater, pearls, finely tailored woolen skirt, and Charles Jourdan boots, she looked the picture of proper Back Bay society.

Later, when we were alone in the ladies' room, I asked her where she got the courage to talk dirty to her man. Jessica blushed and said, "Oh, I practiced in front of a mirror for a month!"

The aspiring fantasy-teller can take a lesson from Jessica, a lady who, despite her impeccable taste and upbringing, developed the confidence to become bold in the boudoir. It wasn't easy for her to learn to speak erotically, but, imagining the rewards, she practiced until she felt comfortable. An avid reader, particularly of women's literature, Jessica had searched out respected authors who tastefully, yet graphically, portrayed sexual encounters. She would then strip down and read those passages aloud to her mirror. After she had accepted the fact that a lady can "talk dirty" to her man without losing her dignity, she had taken the first important step toward ultimate sexual fulfillment. "I may talk dirty," she giggled, "but Nick still insists I'm the sort of girl a man takes home to his mother."

Ladies Do Talk Dirty

"Nice girls don't say those words!" admonished your sweet, well-meaning mother. Perhaps *she* didn't, but *you* are living in a much more liberated society than she ever knew. If you're worried that it's unladylike to talk about sex explicitly and colorfully, just consider what women have been writing and reading over the last twenty years. I remember back in the 50's when Grace Metalious pioneered steamy sex in popular fiction by showing what really went on in the bedrooms of *Peyton Place*. (My girlfriend Cathy and I underlined in red and memorized all the sexy passages while hiding in a closet filled with her mother's lingerie.) Jacqueline Susann pushed the frontiers even further with her *Valley of the Dolls*. Then came Erica Jong's *Fear of Flying* and Anäis Nin's *Delta of Venus* and *Little Birds*. These aren't trashy books, either. Try reading the lovemaking scene in Toni Morrison's award-winning *Tar Baby* without getting turned on!

Last year, 40% of the books sold in the United States were romance novels. But don't bother searching their pages for lily-white virgins whose nipples never harden. No, those Victorian virgins of yesteryear have been replaced by flesh and blood heroines who relish their own sexuality as they live out modern readers' fantasies. Will we women settle for "When Alexandra saw Horace she felt her heart pounding and feared she might faint," when we can have, "When Alexandra saw Horace she felt her nipples harden and decided she'd teach him a few tricks in bed before the evening ended"?

Reading aloud from a juicy novel, particularly from the lovemaking scenes, can help familiarize you with erotic talk. In the secrecy of your own bedroom you can become accustomed to hearing yourself say those words your mother warned you against. Read your favorite pages aloud two or three times. Close your eyes and pretend you and your special man are doing all those wicked, wonderful things!

EXERCISE 3

Required Reading

To get a feeling for how respected authors write about making love you should read as much good, erotic literature as you can get your hands on. Two of my favorites are *The White Hotel* by D.M. Thomas, Pocket Books, March, 1982, pp. 15–29, where you will enjoy reading the sexiest poem I have ever read, and Jerzy Kosinski's *Pinball,* Bantam Books, June 1983, pp. 265–269.

Still more erotic lovemaking is described in Anäis Nin's *Delta of Venus,* Harcourt Brace Jovanovich, 1977, p. 116 (actually you should read the entire book!). A particularly steamy lovemaking scene appears in Judith Krantz's *Mistral's Daughter,* Bantam Books, 1983, pp. 288–289, and the sobering *Executioner's Song* by Norman Mailer, Little, Brown, 1979, pp. 134–135 relates the intimate, sexual side to Gary Gilmore's ill-fated relationship with Nicole Barrett.

Deliciously Dirty

Throughout my adult life I have developed some very close friendships with men, some of whom are quite famous, all of whom are very intelligent. When the occasion arises, we honestly share our experiences with the opposite sex. Hearing about the seduction of Ryan, a male friend shook his head and paid me the highest compliment: "Babe, you are *deliciously* dirty."

The truth is, I have always thought of myself as a highly sexual being, even when I've been pregnant or overweight. And if you are going to start whispering in your man's ear, you'll do everyone a favor by striving to become "deliciously dirty," too. Here are a few tricks and treats to get you started. (And, yes, Mother, I've tried them all.)

Tricks and Treats

- Stand on your balcony or back porch on a windy day, without wearing panties. This is particularly stimulating if you're expecting your lover any moment.
- Go to an X-rated movie alone. When you come home, write a review of the movie. Develop your critical judgment of the erotic scenes.
- Write your man's name on your breast, thighs, or ass with a felt-tip pen. Then show it to him.
- Write the name of an erotic book or magazine on your shopping list and be sure your man sees it. When he asks about it, just smile.
- Go to the next women's club meeting wearing a garter belt, especially if the topic is "Getting Ahead in a Man's World."
- Stand in the mirror with a cucumber between your legs and watch yourself play with it.
- Spray perfume on the light bulbs in your office, bedroom, or living room and take a long whiff whenever you enter the room.
- Casually brush your nipples when you are riding home from work, even if you are on a subway with a hundred people around.
- Curl up comfortably in front of your mirror, shake your head and muss up your hair, and start talking dirty to "him."
- Go to a museum and find paintings of women with bodies similar to yours and admire their beauty.

Sexual Assertiveness Training

Any woman can quickly overcome her hesitancy about "talking dirty" by developing the positive mental attitude I call sexual assertiveness.

Don't confuse sexual assertiveness with aggressiveness; macho men may yearn for romance, but they can feel threatened or used by the domineering Amazon. When I suggest that you become more sexually assertive, I mean that you should refine and master the art of seduction. A shy women may find this difficult at first, particularly if she's been raised in a traditionally submissive role, but even the most conventionally reared woman can learn to deliver a sexual punch that the so-called liberated woman can only envy. How? By telling her lover fantasy stories, of course.

As we saw with Nicholas Weatherbee, many men fall for a versatile woman who can play the demure debutante one minute, the ravenous vixen the next. Never underestimate the element of surprise. Kick off your shyness, be assertive, and open the doors to a new world of joy and fulfillment. Easy for me to say? Sure, but as you'll see, easy for you to learn, too.

Even if you always make love in the missionary position, with the man dominating the action, you can still call the shots in bed. Begin by thinking of yourself not as a sexual object, but as a sexual *objet d'art*. After you've become comfortable talking dirty to your mirror or tape recorder, you can graduate to practicing your sexuality publicly without your man around. Just remember to play it safe.

A friend of mine practiced her sexual assertiveness by dressing up in a finely tailored pair of designer slacks, high-heeled shoes, a form-fitting silk blouse cinched with a wide belt, and a gardenia pinned in her hair. Then she walked through the lobby of New

York's Plaza Hotel. The admiring glances of the well-heeled clientele made her feel like a new woman and gave her the confidence to dress in that same way for her man later that week.

Cotton Undies Are for Nuns

In order to cultivate a sexy appearance, you should experiment with clothing and costumes. Have you ever worn a garter belt, crotchless panties, or nipple-exposing bras? You'll find lots of sources for such items in the Whole Fantasy Catalogue at the end of this book.

But you can start by visiting your favorite store to shop for some expensive sexy lingerie in your man's favorite color. But don't dress for him—dress for yourself. At home you can critically examine your mirror image and strike poses you think look seductive. Study different poses to learn your best angles. If your hair looks drab or your thighs a little flabby, run to a hairdresser, or enroll at the local exercise salon. Once you envision yourself as devastatingly desirable, so will he!

More Tricks and Treats

- Lie down naked in front of your mirror and think about the thrill you felt the first time a boy or man slid his finger into your vagina. Then recreate the scene by describing it aloud, in detail, while sliding your own finger or dildo deep inside. Think about how wonderful it will be to recreate that special thrill as a mature woman with the man you adore.

- Using a mirror, trim your pubic hairs or shave yourself clean. Then massage warm oil all over your vulva. Tell the mirror what it feels like. Get used to talking boldly about your sexual feelings.

Every woman should have an electric vibrator or dildo in her erotic treasure chest. Regardless of the shape or model vibrator you choose, first find a picture of a man who looks like your man (or any man you'd like to take into your bed). Then tape this picture to the corner of your mirror. Be sure to add the right romantic touches: dim lights or flickering candles, a frilly nightgown, soft music on the stereo, and incense or erotic perfume. When you do masturbate, *vocalize* your feelings; tell the imaginary "him" what you want him to do, what you want to do to him, and how it all feels.

Love Sounds

Sound adds a key component to the total sexual environment. I don't mean romantic music or the sound of crashing surf, but the moanings and cries and slippery swishings of enthusiastic lovers.

To fortify your sexual assertiveness, view an X-rated film or a home video cassette that features explicit lovemaking. Once the action commences, pay strict attention to those special sounds that actresses make in their throats—the kittenish squeals of delight, the full, soft moans of pleasure, and the exuberant scream of orgasm. Notice the inflection and timing. Rarely do porn stars talk a "blue streak," but when they do say something they do so for the sexy effect. Can you imitate those noises? Slip on that new lingerie, dab on some expensive perfume in all the right places, and lie back on your bed and practice.

EXERCISE 4

The Pillowtalk Game

Using the "dirty" words your man's Sexual Fantasy Inventory revealed, you can turn talking dirty into a naughty game. Play alone, with a ladyfriend over coffee, or even with your man. He'll laugh, but he'll also marvel at your newfound sexiness.

THE PILLOWTALK GAME

A (Activity)	*B (Your parts)*	*C (His parts)*
touch	lips	tongue
brush	mouth	teeth
rub	finger	fist
massage	tits	cock
fuck	pussy	ass
suck	thigh	knee
lick	foot	calf
stick	ass	balls
___ (add your own)	___ (add your own)	___ (add creative ones)
___	___	___
___	___	___
___	___	___

I've given you the bare bones of a fantasy story. Now you can just fill in the blanks:

"Let's pretend that we went on vacation. After dinner we go back to the room and you began to ______ (A) my ______ (B) with your ______ (C). I felt a tingle deep inside my ______ (B). I ______ (A) my ______ (B) on your ______ (C) while you moaned and begged me to ______ (A) my own ______ (C). In the mirror on the ceiling I admired your ______ (C), but you suddenly began to ______ (A) your ______ (C) on my ______ (B), and I started ______ (A) my own ______ (B). You liked that so much that you asked me to ______ (A) your ______ (C) at the same time. And it felt even better when I began to ______ (A) your ______ (C) with your ______ (C) up my ______ (B). When you asked if I would ______ (A) your ______ (B), I said, 'It's up to you.' Then you ______ (A) your ______ (C) in my ______ (B) and we ______ (A) and ______ (A) until morning."

Now that you've practiced the rhythm and feel of talking sexy, it's time for some serious training. No football player would go to the Superbowl unprepared, so you must develop your talent as cheerleader, quarterback, and wide receiver all rolled into one. After all, you don't want to merely play the game, you want to capture the World Championship.

Training Your Voice

Every aspiring fantasist should include a tape recorder in her toolbox. Since it allows you to practice over and over again until your voice sounds just as appealing as the sexiest actress, nothing will help you get more comfortable quicker than telling fantasy stories. Do a few warm-ups before you actually start recording, perhaps by reading the newspaper or a magazine aloud. Once you've found your ideal level and pitch you can progress to recording sexy passages from books or to your very own first fantasy story. Start slowly with something like this:

"You were a pilot during the war. After blowing three enemy fighter planes out of the sky, you were returning to home base. The thrill of your mission excited you, and you found yourself unzipping your fly and taking out your penis.

"You stroked yourself slowly all the way home until, finally, when you spotted your home base, you beat harder and harder. When you were ready to touch down you took your silk flying scarf from around your neck and beat off into it, feeling the soft silk, so nice and cool against your fiery rod."

Now let's advance to the next step and make believe someone can *actually hear you* telling a fantasy story. To do this, call any telephone number that plays a recording but which does not record messages, like a movie theater, the weather phone, or the time phone. You might whisper this:

"While cruising a country road you ran out of gas in the middle of nowhere and had to start hitching. Eventually you reached a farmhouse and stopped, hoping you could use their phone.

"When no one answered the door you walked around to the back and saw the farmer's daughter bending over a hoe in the garden. Apparently she had not heard you approaching, because she had lifted her skirts up around her waist and was sliding a finger in and out of her pussy. After a few minutes she started to use two fingers, slipping them in and out as she moaned softly.

"Unable to hide your presence any longer, you coughed quietly until she finally saw you. Startled, she stopped playing with herself and she demurely lowered her eyes. You approached her cautiously and offered to hold her while the two of you looked at her garden. Slowly you both sank to the ground. Your left hand found her breast while your right hand raised her skirt. After stroking her thigh for a few moments, you traced a path along the inside of her thigh until you found her moistened patch. Slowly and seductively you entered her with your strong fingers and were surprised to feel the quiver of her orgasm so soon."

If any of your early recordings particularly satisfy you, save them. One day you might want to hand one to your man as he is leaving in the morning.

Learning to Be a Spellbinder

To make her fantasy story even more authentic, Laura decided to perfect an Italian accent. Her boyfriend, Boris, a successful architect, had worked his way through college selling ladies' shoes in an expensive and fashionable Gold Coast Chicago boutique. So Laura chose the shoe store as the setting for Boris's first fantasy story. From her research she knew that Boris adored Sophia Loren, that he had suffered as a shy, scrawny adolescent, disliked dirty words, loved big-breasted women with foreign accents, and yearned to vacation in Mexico.

A born mimic, Laura learned to imitate an Italian accent—groping playfully for words in broken English and gesturing wildly with her hands. She practiced, practiced, practiced until she could get her friends to laugh over her lilting, lyrical imitation of Maria Bellisima, a fictional Italian sex symbol.

Boris would get so excited by Italian accents that Laura could make him hard by simply greeting him at the door with a "Buono Notte," or suggesting that they go to an Italian restaurant where she would order in her Maria accent—a signal to Boris that a night of exuberant frolics has begun.

You can do this, too, even if you have no gift for languages. Just learn a few words of any dialect or accent that stimulates your man, then work them into your repertoire. But don't get too comfortable. Whenever Laura senses Boris's boredom with what she calls an "Italian evening," she tries a little French. There is more than one language of love!

Listen to crafty Laura's favorite fantasy story script:

"*While I was meditating yesterday I had a vision of you as a young college student. You were working at an elegant shoe store to put yourself through school. And on this particular day you were bent over a society matron's foot vainly trying to fit it into a Charles Jourdan pump when you heard someone tap her toe to get your attention. It was Maria Bellisima in a green silk dress that clung so tightly to her breasts, you could tell she wasn't wearing a bra.*

"*Your heart leaped to your throat as you scrambled from the pile of shoe boxes on the floor. The lady you had been helping left in a huff, leaving you alone with Maria. While kneeling humbly, trying hard to ignore her gorgeous legs, you felt yourself getting hard. When you apologized for gripping her ankle too firmly, she said in her beautiful throaty accent, 'Oh no, I like that.' She added that she greatly admired slender young men. 'In fact,' she murmured as she ran her stockinged toe against your thigh, 'you're the nicest young man I've met in a long time.'*

"Her toes brushed your crotch gently, and then she lifted her foot so you could slip it into a stiletto-heeled shoe. Her skirt crept higher and higher until you could see her full thighs. You became so excited that you dropped the shoe. And when you reached to pick it up, Maria whispered, 'For you.' Suddenly she pulled the hem of her skirt into her lap, revealing her pantie-less crotch with her luxurious pubic hair barely concealing her swollen lips. She cocked her head and shot you a smile that froze you into a state of shocked bliss.

"After she bought the shoes, Maria asked you to help her carry the boxes back to her waiting limousine. Sliding into the back of the car, and offering another glimpse of her long legs, she invited you to visit her the following week while she was making a film on location in Puerto Vallarta. 'I leave for airport right now!' she whispered in your ear. 'I'll be waiting!' Then she was gone.

"The following week, you flew to Mexico and rendezvoused, one hot, tropical evening, with the actress in her plush hotel suite. Soon you were lounging in a large room with a view of the beach, daydreaming while Maria dressed for dinner. Listening to her splashing in her bath, you pictured her naked on the deep-pile carpeting at your feet. Moments later she glided into the room with only a towel draped around her waist. 'You like, uh, how you say? Big teets?' She twirled for your inspection, dropping her towel to the

floor. 'You have so beautiful a mouth. You please suck my teet?' she asked. She cupped one full breast and bent to brush the nipple across your lips. You licked and fondled her breasts for an hour while she softly moaned, 'bene, bene.' "

Notice that Laura's fantasy story for Boris does not culminate in intercourse. Why not? Because by the time Laura gets to the part where Maria lies moaning in Boris's arms, Laura has her fist around Boris's erection and can feel him about to ejaculate. "Suck my teet" always pushes Boris's "hot" button, and Laura would rather have him come inside her, so *she*, not Maria, can enjoy the grande finale.

EXERCISE 5

An S.A.T. They Never Gave in High School

This exercise will help you measure your own sexual assertiveness in order to see where you stand now and to see how far you might have to go to think *playfully* of yourself as a "Sexually Sophisticated Siren." Keep track of your answers to the questions in the exercise.

1. If you were lying on a deserted beach and knew that a couple of elderly men were sitting above you on a cliff, you might: A) Make sure your robe was securely tied on. B) Roll over and be sure to expose one breast. C) Strip naked.

2. Imagine yourself at a cocktail party where you're standing on a large mirror with three young men. Would you: A) Wear your sexiest panties? B) Wear no panties at all? C) Have a small tattoo tattooed on your inner thigh?

3. If you went to a wet T-shirt contest, you'd rather be: A) A man. B) A judge. C) The winning contestant.

4. Pretend you're a young married woman whose husband seems uncomfortable or shy with your first attempts at talking dirty. You would: A) Give up. B) Keep trying. C) Tell him the best way to shut you up is to stick his dick in your mouth.

5. Which best describes your own fantasy lover: A) An intelligent lover. B) An animal in bed. C) A "tiger" with a Ph.D. from M.I.T.

6. If you went alone to your twenty-year high school reunion and the captain of the football team (still a gorgeous hunk) asked to take you home, you would: A) Tell him you're in love with another man and monogamous. B) Go parking with him, and this time feel *him* up. C) Tell him you don't want to go home, that you'd rather go to a motel.

7. You have the opportunity to make love with Robert Redford, yet you're concerned about your bulging midriff. Would you: A) Tell him no. B) Suck in your gut while he slides into your bed, and hold your breath all night long. C) Make love to him doggie-style so he can't see your belly.

8. Your perfect lover must possess: A) A large penis. B) Thick, sensuous lips. C) A pelvis that rotates one hundred miles an hour.

9. Your favorite exercise tightens: A) Your belly. B) Your buttocks. C) Your vaginal muscles.

10. You're in Martinique on a beach where all the

women are topless. Would you: A) Feel embarrassed about your black one-piece suit, but keep it on anyway. B) Take your top off too. C) Take your top off and flick at your nipples until they become hard.

11. A man offers you one thousand dollars to make love with another woman. Would you: A) Tell him to get lost. B) Let the woman make love to you without your touching her. C) Go all the way, provided he doubled the offer.

12. If your lover asks you to make love with another man while he watches, would you: A) Ignore the request, hoping that he'll forget about it. B) Find a male friend that you both enjoy, and have a ball. C) Concoct a fabulous fantasy-story that feeds his imagination while you remain true to him.

13. In the past you have made love in interesting, out-of-the-way places. They include: A) The shower. B) Your back yard. C) A crowded parking lot.

14. At least once in your life you have dressed up wearing: A) A garter belt and silk stockings. B) Crotchless panties and a nipple-less bra. C) Edible underwear.

Scoring:
Well, let's see how your scores measure up.
For all "A" answers give yourself 3 points.
For all "B" answers award yourself 5 points.
For all "C" answers you get a magic 10 points.

0–45: It seems you're still a little shy and might need to coax yourself and build your courage. If you feel comfortable at this level, don't feel inadequate, but do try to experiment a bit more boldly.

45–90: Congratulations! You're among the large middle group of women who can become more creative in bed. You should find many pleasing ideas in the rest of this book.

90 or better: You've graduated from intermediate to advanced assertiveness. Prepare to have oxygen available for your lover when you let loose with his fantasy stories.

LESSON 4

Off Broadway

The traditional telltale signs—a lipstick smudge on the fly of his white boxer shorts, a motel key among his loose change—convinced Lacey Marshall that her husband of seven years was having an affair. So she invited his elderly secretary to lunch and soon learned that her husband Gordon was indeed seeing a voluptuous young sales rep for the company. Such a discovery would devastate most wives, but Lacey resolved to fight for her man.

One day Gordon found this mysterious unsigned note in his morning mail: "I love the way you move your body. I bet you're good in bed." Similar anonymous notes began arriving twice a day, each one growing bolder and more explicit. According to Gordon's secretary, whom Lacey had roped into the plot, the letters were really turning the young executive on.

Finally, Gordon's secret erotic admirer invited him to meet her in the flesh, in the lobby of a swank hotel. "You'll recognize me because I'll be wearing a full-length mink coat," read the invitation. Imagine Gordon's surprise when he strolled eagerly into the hotel lobby to find Lacey standing there in mink and high heels. At Gordon's confused look, Lacey discreetly opened her coat to reveal that she was stark naked underneath. "C'mon lover," she whispered, "I've got champagne on ice upstairs."

A few weeks later, Gordon's secretary told Lacey that her boss had abruptly stopped his affair with the sales rep the day after "his wife" surprised him. "You teased him back into your bed," she remarked.

Teasing Your Audience

By now you're probably eager to set the stage for your lover's first fantasy story. Depending on your own sexual assertiveness and on the depth of sexual intimacy already established between you and your man, you can now carefully prepare him for sexual pleasure he may only have dreamed about.

Basically, you can adopt one of two tactics: you either can spring the fantasy on him without warning, as I did with Ryan, or you can approach him more cautiously, gradually warming him up to the idea. Only you can decide what's best for your unique relationship.

Some of the most erotic peaks of my life have been scaled by the man who knew how to talk sexily to me. Perhaps this is why highly intelligent men make such wonderful lovers; they practice the art of verbal seduction as well as the art of actual lovemaking. It works even better for women. Teasing is like foreplay—it sets the stage, establishes a mood, and insures a successful outcome.

The bait for your trap is erotic talk and bold body language, and you must spring it unpredictably. Remember how Lacey's slow-burning fuse exploded in a bang-up surprise! Be receptive to your man's problems, tolerant of his moods, and patient when he irritates you. Take a lesson from Mother Nature. Breeze in like the trade winds, then gradually build up to hurricane force.

Slow and Easy

Perhaps you're an old-fashioned gal who prefers her man in the missionary position for good, straight, loving sex.

My friend Martha, though anxious to begin telling fantasy stories to her boyfriend, Greg, had to make peace with her vision of herself as a lady. Martha is the kind of woman whose hair always looks freshly styled even after two sets of tennis, whose mouth never ever utters a swear word, and who dates a clean-shaven junior executive. She only loosens up in bed when she can use the excuse of having had one drink too many. Given the lazy warmth of her relationship with her boyfriend, Martha chose to work up to her opening night gradually, especially since her newly developed boldness might alarm her man. Listen to her advice:

- "I told my first fantasy story away from home, on a special, romantic vacation weekend. Of course, I had packed some sexy, revealing lingerie for the trip."

- "When I brought breakfast to him in bed the first morning, I didn't cover up my nightie with a robe, but let him feast his eyes on me in a comfortable situation. By not wearing the traditional cover-up, I gave him an unmistakably sexual signal. Later, I casually allowed a strap to fall down, exposing a breast, then asked him to fix it."
- "During lovemaking recently I tried something mildly new and daring (for me!)—I stroked his penis after intercourse and planted a little kiss on its tip."
- "One night I left my lover this thank you note stashed under his pillow: 'You fuck like an angel.' It was easier for me to *write* dirty before I *talked* dirty."
- "Sometimes I let my hands wander onto my breasts while he is watching me. I even let them linger there. The other night I fondled a nipple until it became hard and then smiled at him and said, 'Just thinking about you drives me crazy.' "
- "He hardly believed his eyes when I undressed in front of him after we had attended a church supper, revealing that I been wearing a lacy black garter belt."

You can see how carefully Martha set the stage for her fantasy story by slowly revealing the sexually assertive side to her nature. Yet even with her subtle teasing, Martha's boyfriend was completely surprised when she finally launched her attack.

Noting that their most pleasurable sex occurred

during their infrequent vacations, Martha reserved a suite for a long weekend at San Francisco's venerable Mark Hopkins Hotel.

"Greg had business in San Francisco, so I told him to take his time and meet me in the disco bar at the hotel, after dinner. I went on a go-for-broke binge, buying a clinging black jersey dress, and a lime green baby-doll negligee to set off my red hair and green eyes. Then I treated myself to 'the works' at an expensive salon: a permanent, facial, manicure, and pedicure. . . . I felt like a million bucks."

Back at the hotel, Martha ordered up flowers and a bottle of Dom Perignon champagne, dined on salad nicoise and a jumbo shrimp cocktail, and then bathed in bath oil before donning her new dress.

"When I looked in the mirror, I hardly recognized myself, which is just what I wanted. I went down to find the disco already jumping—full of business people and singles. Since Greg hadn't arrived, I accepted a drink from a handsome young man who openly admired my braless, full breasts."

While Martha was dancing to a slow song with this stranger, Greg arrived tired from a long business session and was just a little high on two martinis.

"At first Greg's eyes skimmed the room looking for me, but when he finally recognized me, his eyes almost fell out of their sockets. Disengaging myself, I walked over to him, saying, 'Hey handsome, where've you been all my life?' He tried to kiss me, but I pushed him away. 'Let's pretend we're strangers,' I said. 'You can't try to pick me up until midnight.' He shook his head but looked amused and played along with the game. We both danced with other people for a couple of hours. When he finally approached my table at the stroke of twelve, I whispered in his ear, 'Let's fuck.'

Well, we barely made it into the room before he tore off my dress. It was the best sex we ever had, so we now regularly schedule a 'vacation' every few months just to keep the spark in our relationship and a wild tiger in my tank."

Mildly Seasoned

During my research I had the pleasure of meeting Vivien, a lovely middle-aged dentist from Detroit, who considers herself a woman of the 80's. Vivien has a healthy sexual appetite; she likes to act like a cool professional in the office and a brazen hussy in the bedroom. Throughout the liberation of the 70's Vivien developed into a more sexually assertive woman, initiating sex when she felt the urge, buying a drawer full of naughty lingerie, and peppering her social conversation with sexy language. And Vivien does not feel self-conscious when party conversation turns to sex. Her husband is not surprised when she joins him in the shower for a soapy lovemaking interlude, nor does he hesitate to slip a porno flick into their VCR when he knows the kids are sleeping at a friend's house. Although she describes herself as monogamous, Vivien harbors secret sexual fantasies about some of her younger male patients and she has even occasionally masturbated while thinking of them.

When I suggested that she introduce fantasy stories into her lovelife, she eagerly embraced the idea and agreed to keep me informed of her progress. Here's how she set the stage:

- "First I started writing out cute dirty jokes and slipping them into my husband's briefcase."
- "Another time I cut the nipples out of my bra and

wore it that way under a sheer, but not transparent, blouse when we went out for dinner."

- "I asked my husband to autograph my bare belly and the inside of my thigh with a felt-tip pen. Actually, I picked up this tip from an overseas stewardess who told me she loves to tease a new lover by letting him decorate her body with washable children's watercolors. One guy had used her pubic hair for the beard on a perfect Sigmund Freud caricature."
- "When we went to see a Paul Newman movie I told my husband, 'He may be good looking, but I bet your cock is bigger.' "
- "I asked my husband if he'd like to borrow *my* latest copy of *Penthouse*."
- "After calling him at his office, I pretended to be an obscene phone-caller, saying 'I want you to come on my tits,' before I hung up. You should have seen the expression on my husband's face when he came home that night."
- "When he left for Atlanta on a business trip, I called him in his hotel room and asked him to take out his penis and play with it while I played with myself. 'I was watching a dirty movie, and I started thinking about you,' I said."
- "On the day I chose to tell him his first fantasy story, I woke up before him, curled up head-to-foot, and awakened him with my lips grazing his penis."

The daughter of one of my close friends put Vivien's advice into practice. Sammy Jo, the daughter, is a gorgeous, slim business school student who had had a casual attitude about uninvolved sex while she was an undergraduate. But deep down lovely Sammy Jo felt quite insecure and feared intimacy because she'd seen many of her girlfriends get hurt. Now, for the first time in her life, she had fallen head over heels in love.

Her dream man was Cary, a stunningly handsome marathon runner from Oregon with whom she had moved in shortly after they met. But a problem arose. Sammy Jo, in spite of her own brains and beauty, felt quite jealous whenever Cary left Oregon to compete in races. From experience she knew that distance runners made great lovers and attracted lots of track star groupies. When I suggested that she try fantasy stories as a way of keeping her man, Sammy Jo eagerly agreed to try. Seven months later, Cary and Sammy Jo met with me over dinner the day after the New York City Marathon. With a pear-shaped diamond sparkling on her engagement finger, Sammy Jo cajoled Cary into telling me how she teased him into her net.

"First, I noticed Sam eating salad and barbecued chicken with her fingers and then lick them clean in this slow, sucking kind of way," said Cary. "I wondered what had happened to her boarding school manners. It really got to me when she rhythmically slid her middle finger in and out of her lips with her big brown eyes staring straight into my soul. After dinner she behaved quite normally, but I couldn't get that image out of my mind.

"Soon she started asking me questions about my childhood, something no woman had ever done; that really drew us closer together. Then, the night I packed my bags for the Boston Marathon, a lingerie catalogue mysteriously appeared in my athletic bag. When I asked Sam if she had ordered a Halloween costume, she smiled and murmured, 'No, just a tricky treat for some lucky man.' That made me nervous, and I worried during the flight the next day whether she planned to play around while I was gone.

"You can imagine my surprise when two days later I received a letter describing in detail how I had made love to her the night before I left.

"Finally, she hit me with the *pièce de résistance:* a hasty note from her saying she'd decided to join me in Boston. This startled me. She usually avoided major races because they made me so keyed up. Inside the note she had inserted a polaroid photograph of herself in which she was clearly masturbating. When she arrived the next day I demanded she tell me who had taken that picture. 'Silly,' she laughed. 'Don't you remember our camera has a delayed exposure?' "

"Frankly, her behavior baffled me until, finally, the night after the Boston race, she told me an incredible fantasy story. Actually, I'm glad she set me up the way she did. Without any warning, it would have scared the hell out of me."

Not only did intelligent, caring Sammy Jo warm up her man with exquisitely timed teasing, she also used the lingerie catalogue, letter and photo to prepare him for the big event. Her approach helped *her* get used to talking dirty, but more importantly, it went a long way toward eliminating her man's fears and converted his initial shock into delight. Take care to work up to your story gradually. One woman I know released such a pent-up explosion of lust from her husband that it took her two days to convince him she had not picked up her new tricks from another man.

Sometimes, however, you don't have time to set the stage before telling a fantasy story to your lover. If you meet a special gentleman by chance, but feel constrained by time (particularly if you are on vacation) and want to seduce him quickly, you still can do it with dignity and class. Consider the following story about a Florida man I met.

Hunter Hardison, a suave sophisticated gentleman in his late fifties, operates an art gallery in the posh Florida resort town of Key Biscayne. With a high population of widows and divorcees, it's a bachelor's paradise with an endless supply of eager women outdoing each other to snatch up a new mate. Hunter told me:

"I had been walking down the beach one Sunday and stopped at an outdoor bar on the beach for a piña colada. That's where I met Greta, a stunningly handsome woman in her early sixties. After several drinks and a lively, intellectually stimulating conversation, I suggested that Greta come to my place for dinner that night.

"She arrived promptly at 7 o'clock with a superb bottle of wine and the most amazing corkscrew I have ever seen: its handle a life-sized mahogany model of an erect penis. Throughout dinner Greta wanted to know all about me, quite a switch from the typical widow who can't stop describing the final months of her late husband's incurable bout with cancer. We made quiet love later that night and agreed to meet again in three days.

"When she returned, she asked to see my watercolor collection. During the tour, she got a faraway look in her eyes and began talking so softly that I had to bend down to hear her!

"Suppose we could walk into one of these paintings. 'Which would you choose?' she asked. 'The one with three young women lying naked in the forest surrounded by flowers? Look, that's you behind the tree

watching the girls perform a sexual ballet. Though they're all virgins, each has mastered the art of sex without penetration. Don't you love that idea? One exquisite nubile blonde dances joyfully for you while another lightly brushes your naked back with her nipples. The third skips to the dancer and begins to caress her body with innocent kisses.' "

Slender Greta then took Hunter to bed, lighting a single candle in whose dim glow she resembled one of the girls in the painting. "She amazed me again, looking not a day over thirty, dancing with the obscene corkscrew, teasing her clitoris, but never actually inserting it all the way. She saved that for me!"

Recently, Hunter sent me a postcard from Mykonos where they had moored Greta's chartered yacht for several days. "We've commissioned an artist to recreate Greta's first fantasy. We'll send you a print for your collection," read the card.

Wild and Wonderful

During a much-needed vacation last summer I struck up a conversation on the beach with Yvette, a dazzling, blond, documentary film producer from Beverly Hills who unabashedly described herself to me as the "total" woman. "To hell with 'aural sex,' " she laughed, "I call it mind fucking." Most of us don't know women like Yvette, but they do exist—sleek, hip, self-pampered beauties who appear to have the world (and a dozen or so millionaires) on a string.

"Fantasy stories?" she chuckled, "I've been doing that for years!" When I asked her to share some of her secret techniques with my readers, she agreed. Although her approach may seem a little extreme for most of us, she does have some interesting ideas.

"When I *do* wear a bra, you can be sure it never has nipples," she began. "At least once a week my lover of the moment and I get it on while watching porno video cassettes. I collect outrageous lingerie and the only time I wear cotton panties is when I have a vaginal infection. Whenever I find a really open guy I give him a copy of *The Story of O* and ask him to read it aloud to me.

"Since I own lots of video equipment, I usually offer to film our lovemaking sessions. My men have come to expect wild, hot sex from me; they *know* they can never shock me or outfuck me. So what do I do when I'm really interested in a guy? How do I set him up for what you call fantasy stories? Easy. I start directing the conversation more toward him. I become the best listener he's ever met. From the minute he opens his mouth, I maintain eye contact with him, even if he rambles on for hours. I let him feel my whole universe revolves around him."

The Male Animal

My father was fond of saying, "Women! You can love 'em but never understand 'em!" Well that applies to the complex modern man, too. While researching this book I was occasionally surprised to find some men actually threatened by the idea that a woman—not just any woman, but his *own* woman—would express her deepest sexual feelings. Men can sometimes react with fear and anger to women who change their sexual patterns without warning. Let's analyze three men who told me that they responded quite differently to sexually assertive women. Their unique personalities demand strikingly different approaches.

Lighting the Slow Fuse

Most of us have encountered a man like Parker—our first subject—an upright pillar in his community who volunteers every summer to coach the Little League team, always pays his bills on time, dresses conservatively, and never swears in front of women (and in fact, seldom swears when he's with the boys). His neatly trimmed hair, conservative suits, and quiet neckties portray the ultimate in quiet, conservative stability. Parker is the type of man you would expect to be levelheaded; he's the neighbor you would ask to watch your house while you were out of town. Of course, he's steadfastly monogamous and was probably a virgin (technically) until he met the ideal potential mate in college. When he finally married his dream girl, he launched a career in insurance, started a family, and bought a comfortable home in the suburbs.

Parker, like any red-blooded American male, may look twice at a stunning blonde in a tight sweater and may even imagine her naked, but he never pictures himself in bed with her. Does he sound boring? Well, don't underestimate him, because Parker became an ardent, exciting lover after his wife learned how to ignite his fuse. If Parker sounds like the man you wish to entice, I must caution you to go very, very slowly, taking into account his conservative nature. You might benefit from these tips from Parker's wife:

- Point out an attractive couple in a restaurant, saying, "I wonder if they make love as well as we do."
- Tell him an X-rated movie had your girlfriend jumping all over her husband for two weeks.

- Change to a more sultry, musky perfume, and rub some on the collar of his shirt.
- Tell him that the novel his mother recommended you read contains some very dirty passages and that you enjoyed them.
- Loll around in your bra and panties some hot night and then ask him to fan you with a newspaper. (Parker's wife found her husband stripping her completely, heating her up rather than cooling her off.)
- Take a belly dancing course and write his name on your belly before you entertain him.
- Leave the panties you've worn all night on top of his pillow.

If your man is like Parker, be sure to complete his Sexual Fantasy Inventory thoroughly. Then study it carefully to expose the startling news. Men like Parker often harbor strong, but deeply hidden fantasies. Gloria was shocked, then thrilled, to discover what would excite *her* Parker.

"Black women?!" she exclaimed. "Imagine, a straight guy from Walla Walla, Washington, wanting to screw Diana Ross and then steal her undies! Well, after I got over my shock I said, 'What the hell,' and bought a half-dozen of her albums. Night after night I practiced before he came home from work, learning to sway my hips suggestively to her music, ending in a slow, seductive striptease.

"It took some courage to do it in front of him over cocktails one night, but when I had stripped down to my new leopard-skin panties and bra, lip-synching 'Ain't No Mountain High Enough,' I could tell he was excited. His reaction made me bolder. After tossing off the underwear, I turned out the lights and curled up naked in his lap. We ended up making love before dinner, right on the living room floor. And just to put the perfect final touch on it all, I tucked the underwear into the breast pocket of Parker's Harris tweed jacket he wore to the office the next day."

Lighting a Shorter Fuse

If your man has a shorter fuse than Parker, he may be more like Dave, who was the big man on campus. He was a practical joker, fun-loving, carefree, and got decent grades in college but definitely saw it as a last chance to have a good time. Once out of school, he landed a great job as a salesman, explored a wide variety of women, bought a snazzy car, and decorated his nice big-city apartment.

Dave often brags of his sexual conquests and likes to describe himself as a ladies' man. In bed, Dave is not embarrassed about asking a woman to go down on him, and he eagerly reciprocates; he loves to make love and prefers you to chocolate mousse as dessert at the end of a dinner date. But take heed: underneath the jovial facade often lies a repressed little boy waiting for the right woman to satisfy his unfulfilled sexual appetite. One woman who had set her sights on Dave used these tips to make him her own exclusive gourmet:

- Mention a dream about his old college girlfriend in which you and she took turns making love to him.
- Tell him you took a poll of your girlfriends and that they all imagine he's a wild guy in bed.

- Say it's okay if he doesn't get hard after drinking too much beer. Say that sometimes you'd rather play with yourself and let him watch.
- Slip a pair of your silk panties around his legs while he's sleeping. (Dave's lady taught him the joy of masturbating into silk panties while she watches.)
- Rub ice cubes on his cock and balls the next time you're in bed together. Or suck him off with cold champagne or warm tea in your mouth. (Dave enjoyed having an ice cube rubbed on his anus while screwing his lady.)
- Confide to him that you wish his old flame would walk in and catch the two of you fucking your brains out.
- Dip your hand into your pussy the next time he comes inside you, then lick the juices off your fingers.

My friend Sharon, a successful fashion consultant, met a man very much like Dave. When she learned from his Sexual Fantasy Inventory that her man had exhibitionist fantasies and had dreamed of owning a Lotus sports car, she created this wonderful fantasy story for him:

"Yesterday I was modeling at the Auto Show and, as I was leaving, I spotted a jazzy, red Lotus. Funny thing, the man who was selling it looked just like you. Driving home, I found myself imagining you were at the wheel driving me out to the Hamptons one hot summer night. I imagined I had pulled your cock from your trousers the minute we left my place, and that I stroked it all the way there. Well, you had a blissful

smile on your face until that tractor-trailer truck pulled alongside us at the stop sign. Did I let go of you? Not for a second. In fact, the minute the light turned green, I went down on you. You were so hot and excited, I knew you were going to come in a minute. So what did I do? I pulled off my silk panties and stroked you to climax with them until you came in strong, pulsing throbs. Weren't you embarrassed when the truck passed us, tooting its horn!"

Dynamite

But what if your guy is wilder than Parker or Dave? What if your guy is more like Todd—a keg of dynamite waiting for just the right match to explode his passion.

I met Todd many years ago when I visited Washington, D.C. He was a well-known Defense Department spokesman who had retired from government service to take a position as an executive with a major aerospace corporation. He had lived all over the world and had spent many vacations in Bangkok and Hong Kong brothels learning every trick in the *Kama Sutra*. Countless wealthy women (including many of the glittering socialites and heiresses in Washington and New York) longed to get their hands on this handsome man. But worldly Todd was smart enough to know that no amount of fame and fortune could guarantee mutual satisfaction in bed.

A few years later I met Todd again at a convention hotel in Miami. "I want you to meet my new bride!" he said.

Jennifer, his bride, turned out to be a petite brunette with a perky face and figure, a warm smile, and a friendly manner. But she was hardly a showstopper. Taking her aside, I asked if she'd tell me how she snagged such a sought-after bachelor. Luckily for me, Jennifer loosened up after a few drinks and revealed her technique.

"Of course, I dangled some flashy bait in front of his eyes before I hooked Todd. But he bit the bait so hard, I had no trouble reeling him in." You may want to take Jennifer's advice:

- Next time that you're together, tell him you want to tie him up with satin ribbons. Do so, and then straddle his body, standing up so he can see but not touch your pussy. Use a long feather or riding crop to gently stroke his most sensitive parts. When he's ready to explode, untie him and run off to hide in a closet. Let him fuck you among your perfumed clothes.
- Tell him about the time you had sex with another woman, and her brother caught you in the act. Have him tell *you* what happened next.
- Shave your pussy while he watches.
- Film him masturbating. Then tell him you're going to show it at your next bridge party.
- Massage him for hours with exotic, fragrant oils, and play Balinese music in the background. (Since Todd had traveled in Thailand, Jennifer decided to surprise him by draping her bedroom in the luxurious silken fabrics of the Far East. Then she dressed herself like the Asian women whose favors he had enjoyed.)

Jennifer's advice may be a bit exotic for some of us, but men like Todd eat it up. I sat there transfixed as Jennifer related the ultimate fantasy tale that had landed her man. Here's what she whispered in Todd's ear:

"You were in India uncrating a cageful of Bengal tigers. You could tell the female was in heat, because she kept licking her hot, swollen vagina. Growling and straining, she arched her back toward you. You unzipped your trousers and began pulling on your penis. The tigress lay down, coyly swaying, her tail raised high as if inviting you to penetrate her.

"Just then you heard me call out your name, and you spun around to see me draped in a tiger skin, sliding my fingers into my pussy. 'Which would you fuck?' I asked, as I swayed my hips to imitate the wild cat. She was purring now, rolling on her back and clawing the air. I began to pant and purr, myself. 'Which will you fuck?' I teased. And you said, 'Both!' "

Shocking? Perhaps. But this story touched the heart of Todd's sexual response. And now when Jennifer wants her man, all she has to do is purr!

Eliminating His Fears

This exercise will help you reassure your man that he's the unique object of your sexual attention:

- After you invite your man to autograph your thigh, insist you would never allow another man to do this.
- If you call him while he's away on a business trip, your horniness in his absence might make him nervous. Tell him you're sleeping with a pair of his shorts or his shirt on.

- If he construes your buttoning your top button as withholding sexual favor, tell him exposing your flesh to him turns you on so much that if you don't you're afraid you'll rape him in the Howard Johnson's parking lot.
- If you've left a photograph for him to see of two women making love together, tell him you'd only do that to turn him on.

Tease, Then Please

Teasing, when not handled properly, can sometimes seem cruel. And while we want to ease our lovers to the brink of a sexual cliff, we don't want to unnecessarily frustrate them.

So if you decide to follow the tips for teasing, do not leave your man hanging unfulfilled. If you play games but don't really want to follow through, he will quickly lose trust *and* interest.

When Martha found herself separated from her man for two weeks while he fulfilled his National Guard obligations, she sent him photographs of herself, first fully clothed, then without her top, then in her underwear, and finally nude. She arranged for him to receive the pictures in order, along with short love notes. When he came home, they spent a long, lazy morning in bed with the phone off the hook.

Vivien made a lunch date with her man at an elegant restaurant to which she wore an expensive silk blouse and no bra. After the waiter brought the first course, she flashed her breasts and her lover nearly choked on his soup. When they got into his car she flashed him again, taking enough time to allow him to read a love message she had written in a felt-tip pen across her breasts. They ran straight home to bed.

LESSON 5

Opening Night

"Let me tell you a story," I whispered, voice purring like a sensuous cat in heat, the scent of my Opium perfume intoxicating him from between my breasts.

"The other night while you were out of town I played with myself while looking at your photograph."

My lover of three years looked shocked. "You did what?"

Undaunted, I continued. "I played with myself while I fantasized about fucking you." A puzzled look crept across his face. "What brought this on?" he asked.

I knew he admired our tall, blond Norwegian landlady, Bambi. "I made believe I was watching you fuck Bambi," I responded.

A lightbulb seemed to snap on in his head. "Oh Liane! Now I see what you're up to. You're trying to trap me into confessing that I've been cheating on you. Well, forget it. I'm not getting caught in Liane's web!"

Had I been a novice fantasy story-teller his reaction might have prompted me to abandon the attack or, worse, start a fight. But armed with the knowledge I'd gleaned from his Inventory, I pressed on.

Kneeling on our satin sheets, I cupped his head in my hands and stared at him. "Listen," I said, sliding my arm under his head, "let me finish. In my fantasy Bambi was wearing a transparent negligee and you were taking her doggie-style in our bed."

He let out a soft sigh. "You're nuts," he chided. Yet I saw him twitch and begin to harden. I grasped him firmly and continued. "Play with me while I tell you the rest of my fantasy." I pulled his cock in a slow rhythm while I went on. Periodically he would protest that I must have lost my mind, but his rigid cock told me I was perfectly sane.

"Bambi's large breasts were swaying as you slammed into her from behind, and she was screaming for you to give it to her harder and deeper. You loved the way her firm ass met your belly as you pounded away, pumping like a jackhammer. You couldn't see me watching you from the doorway. While you kept hurling yourself into her, I opened my kimono and let my hands wander from my stiff nipples to my slickening pussy. In fact, I fingered my clit just like you're doing now."

He momentarily paused and shook his head. "How many fingers did you use?" he inquired. His forefinger rested on my clit.

"One," I said.

He slid two fingers deep inside me. "Tell me the truth."

"Two."

All three of his long surgeon's fingers pressed into my core.

"Three." I was beginning to get so excited I was afraid I wouldn't be able to finish my story. So I pulled away and rested my cheek against his erection. While I planted little kisses along the shaft ("Oh you're so *big!") he closed his eyes and groaned.*

"You reached around to hold her swaying breasts in your hands while I pulled on my own nipples, matching your caresses move for move," I continued. "I guess I got carried away and began to moan, because you suddenly stopped and turned your head to see me standing there."

At this point I swallowed his cock, which quivered and climaxed in the strongest series of throbs I'd ever felt.

The moral of this story? Don't let your man's initial fears or protests derail your fantasy train. Pile on the coal, build up a full head of steam. Remember the "little engine that could."

When the Irresistible Force Meets an Immovable Object

Earlier I warned that you may have to take steps to help your man eliminate his fears when you first begin spinning fantasy stories. Why? Hearing you tap his rich, previously buried sources of erotic stimulation may surprise and even frighten him. It would be only natural for him to initially try to shut off the source of discomfort, even if the results of that discomfort can only lead to pleasure. He may feel that you are about to unleash a wild animal, that the restraints with which he has harnessed his sexual freedom may fall away. He may even be afraid that his abandonment—never fully released before—may disappoint you. Oh, but you *know* that the results will only achieve a higher sexual and emotional intimacy between you, so you must try to convince him.

Take it slowly. Try to see any setbacks, such as his initial shock or reticence, as opportunities to seize. Here are some tips on how to be charmingly irresistible:

- Don't laugh at him! Be tender, and cradle him closely. Say, "Ssshh! I'm serious, I *need* to tell you this."
- If he tries to drown you out by turning on the television or stereo, switch to visual stimulation. Curl up next to him and begin to stroke his chest or thigh (or both!). Say, "Okay, I'll just pretend that you're listening."
- Keep him warm. Pull a nice down-filled comforter around the two of you and make him feel snug and cozy in your nest.
- Make sure no one can hear you. *Whisper* in his ear! Caress his penis when you begin his fantasy story. What man can roll away from something he likes so much?
- Tell him you have a cramp and that you'il stop talking only if he agrees to massage you to a climax. When he begins to touch you, start whispering again.
- Remember what Shakespeare wrote: "Methinks

the lady doth protest too much." When your man says, "No," he really means, "Yes!"

- If he still says that he wants you to stop, stop. Go to your dressing table (making sure he can see you) and slowly massage scented oils on your body, taking time on your breasts and between your legs. Visually stimulate him until he begs you back to bed.

- If you've completed his Sexual Fantasy Inventory and thought you'd detected the right clues but it appears that you haven't, temporarily drop the fantasy story and return to your investigative reporting, paying strict attention to detail. Your particular fantasy story, not the technique itself, may be at fault.

Sometimes the fact that you have overlooked an important detail (*new* panties, not worn ones, or a *sailboat* rather than a power launch) can distract your man enough to disturb his responses. It never hurts to admit a setback as long as you don't let it put out the fire in your coal box.

As my own love affair with Ryan progressed I learned to elicit his help in creating fantasy stories. I watched him read the newspaper and made mental notes about the stories he would read aloud to me. When we shopped for *his* cologne, I carefully noted the scent he finally chose—spice versus musk, and heavy versus light. One night I rubbed his cologne all over my body before I began to woo him with a tale of lust. In a wacky way, he was really making love to himself. On one occasion, he caught me watching him test the firmness of a melon in the supermarket. He winked and said, "I can't wait to see how your going to weave this into a story tonight."

I didn't make him wait. While we were standing alone in the produce section, I chose two melons, plucked a long, green banana from a bunch, and unwrapped a roll of toilet paper in our cart. Arranging the melons and the toilet paper roll so that they simulated a woman's body, I teased the hole in the tube with the long, curving banana. "Oh, Liane, what if someone sees you?" he said. But he stood there watching and finally laughed, saying, "You're crazy, baby. One of these days I'm going to rip off your clothes and fuck you on the meat counter." I wish!

You might take my tale of the melons as an example of how to turn any event into a source for fantasy stories. But if you're like most women who've learned my techniques, you've probably already begun telling your man his first fantasy story. In fact, if the results have run true to form, you've probably told him two or three.

But despite the spice that has begun to flavor sex with your man, are you beginning to worry that you might soon run out of fresh ingredients? Not to worry, dear. Just open your eyes and ears to the rich world around you. Can you use the tent he almost bought at the sporting goods store? One woman crawled inside the display and unbuttoned her blouse, telling her man that they could camp out in Macy's. What about the squirrel collecting nuts on your lawn? Your tail's bushy, too.

Searching for Buried Treasure: Fantasy Sources

Go back to his Sexual Fantasy Inventory. Virtually every item there offers a fantasy story source. Heroes, cars, music, vacation—all these can build into dozens upon dozens of lusty stories. Grab your divining rod and hit the trail:

- You visit a coffee house and choose an exotic blend of beans. Tonight make up a story about Juan Juarez and the naked Brazilian cuties who pluck the ripe berries.
- You're kneading dough to make your man's favorite coffee rolls, but this time you instead fashion an enormous cock and balls. Put a little white frosting on its tip.
- The eleven o'clock news reports a man who has eighteen wives in different towns. Why not be all those eighteen different women for your one man?
- Go to a movie, play, opera, or sporting event. While he watches the action observe him, noting what prompts his applause. Later, in bed, put him in the middle of the action; make him the lover in the movies, the broad-shouldered tenor, the flashy hockey player. Take note of a particularly attractive woman in the audience and point her out to your man. Later, in bed, bring her into his imagination. But you'll be in his arms.
- Read any best-selling novel in his favorite genre, be it mystery, science fiction, war, cowboy, or western. Then mimic the plot, weaving him in as the hero.
- Scan the newspaper, paying attention to the entertainment section. Look for ads promoting belly dancing contests, wet T-shirt contests, golf tournaments, etc. Then incorporate them into his bedtime stories.
- Underline blurbs in the "Personals" section of magazines and newspapers that advertise hot, horny maidens. Then hand him one saying, "I wrote that for you." In fact, one bold bombshell

placed this steamy ad in her local paper: "Dear Joe: juicy lady seeks hardened veteran for war games."

- The next time you fly together ask him to pick out the prettiest stewardess. Then add her to your collection of "other women."
- If he exclaims about someone breaking a world's record, work it into a fantasy. Of course, *he's* the record breaker!
- When he tells you about a great guy he met during a business meeting, bring that man and his girlfriend into a make-believe strip-poker game in one of your stories.
- Shop for sexy underwear and buy a pair of panties that will fit him. Cut a hole in front for his cock, then slip them on him after you've tied his wrists and ankles to the bedposts with velvet cords.
- Notice how the design has been changed on this year's model of his fantasy car. Discuss it with him. He'll be surprised that you notice such details. Or go to the annual auto show and have him take your picture next to a red Ferrari. Brenda actually stole the gearshift knob from a classic '57 Chevy and used it later to masturbate in front of her man, making car engine sounds when she climaxed.
- Rewrite the Chairman's letter in your man's company's annual report, directing it to all the women employees. And paste your man's picture over the Chief Executive Officer's face.
- Full-color advertisements provide a rich, rich source, particularly if there's a woman in the

picture. Just find something that interests your man, rip it out of the magazine, and paste over some original copy. Remember Yvette? She turned an innocent ad for a new body shampoo in a family oriented magazine into an erotic experience for her man.

Yvette's lover Drake had fantasized about watching Yvette make it with his raquetball partner, Duke, and jokingly called his penis a "whistle." So Yvette edited the shampoo ad to read:

Bawdy Body Shampoo

With Pussylather Shampoo you can really get your whistle clean. Imagine the soft, silky foam as you rub your chest against your lover's tits, her fingers circling your whistle.

Since Pussylather's organic, your ladylove can play "Yankee Doodle Dandy" all night long, with the extra added benefit of washing out her filthy mouth with soap.

Yvette went further and taped a penis head cut from *Playgirl* over the shampoo bottle's nozzle. When Drake agreed to take a shower with her, she whipped up a concoction of safflower oil and lemon juice (both natural and edible!) which she used instead of the Pussylather.

Props, Costumes, and Decorations

Some men need a visual stimulation along with their aural sex. To better understand this, take a long hard look at the photographs and advertisements in any gentleman's magazine. Don't they all contain props that set off the woman's naked body like a setting displays a jewel? Often the models wear high heels and garter belts with matching silk stockings. Some of the sexiest photographs hide key parts of the body with the filmiest of negligees, while others offer exotic costumes, candlelit hotel rooms, or luxurious forest, mountain, or ocean scenes.

The best stripper I ever saw wore classic preppy clothes. Preppy? Absolutely. More than one man out there has fantasized about screwing the prim and proper girl next door. A plaid skirt, button-down shirt, monogrammed pullover sweater, saddle shoes, bobby socks, cotton panties, and a cloth bra can drive a man as wild as can a satin and lace negligee. Add to your erotic prop collection the costumes and props that appear in at least two issues of *Playboy* and *Penthouse*. (A clever seamstress or craftswoman can make them herself.)

Whether you choose to begin fantasy storytelling using props, or wish to save them for more advanced sessions, these accessories will help make your illusions seem real. And you may be surprised to find that they turn you on, too!

Don't leave your man off your prop list. Does he don a certain costume for Halloween parties? If not, talk him into doing so. Does he dream of playing Tarzan, a fireman, or even a woman? (No, this doesn't mean he's gay.) One doctor's wife told me that her husband, otherwise a straight-arrow guy who washes his hands before and after sex, turns their basement into an elaborate fun house at Halloween and outfits himself in an elaborate Dracula costume. "After the kids stop trick-or-treating, I pull some tricks from my sleeve," she said. "I strip naked in the bat cave and suck him off with his Dracula teeth in my mouth.

That's the only time he forgets to wash his hands."

Your props can also include pictures of his fantasy car, fantasy vacation spot, or fantasy woman. For example, ever since childhood, I dreamed of seeing the mighty Matterhorn. Knowing that my then lover, Josh, an avid hiker, planned to whisk me to the Swiss Alps for a summer vacation, I began dreaming about finally scaling the Matterhorn. For weeks I fantasized about making love to Josh in the mountain's shadow at dusk and I began embroidering this fantasy story with this in mind.

During the first two weeks in Switzerland we hiked throughout the countryside with the Matterhorn seldom out of sight. My thighs became slim and tightly muscled, and my sexual stamina soon reached its peak. Eventually we checked into a charming little hotel in Zermatt called Alpenrose, the bay window of which framed the mountain of my dreams. The room was tastefully furnished with antique oak furniture, and the high feather bed was positioned so we could lie on an intricate patchwork quilt and stare at the Matterhorn, which changes appearance as the sun sails through the sky from dawn to dusk. On an overcast day it looks quite foreboding.

After enjoying excellent, straight sex the first night, I sprang my fantasy story on the second afternoon, during which dark thunderheads occasionally cast the mountain from bright and inspiring to gloomy and threatening.

Josh was restless and impatient to hit the trail, lacking interest in anything but his Swiss Alpine Club topography maps. Fastened to one of his maps with a paper clip he found the last of a series of notes I had begun giving him as we prepared for this trip. It said, "Later, when we're in bed, ask me to tell you the old Swiss fairy tale about the Matterhorn." Josh handed me the note and said, "Okay, maybe it'll help me relax. But let's have some hot chocolate brought up first."

As we waited for the chocolate to arrive, I gave Josh a bath, not a sexually stimulating soaping, but a loving, motherly scrubbing. After toweling him dry, I massaged some Edelweiss-scented oil into his muscular calves and thighs. And after wolfing down the sweet chocolate, I drew back the thick, luxurious quilt on the plush feather bed and wrapped Josh securely in my arms to tell him his fantasy story.

"*Once upon a time,*" *I began,* "*there were two lusty young men who lived in the shadow of the Matterhorn. They were the sons of a mountaineer who had guided many climbers to the summit. Their names were Hans and Joshua. They were only a year apart in age and as close as brothers could be.*

"*One day they set out on the trail together and after three hours of climbing reached the Hornlii Hutte, two-thirds of the way up the Zermatt face of the mountain. Summer had ended, and few climbers were attempting the trail. Hans and Joshua loved the peace and solitude, the joy of being alone together with their great love of the mountain.*

"*When they reached the hut, Heidi, a cheerful, big-busted, and heavily-muscled girl of about twenty-two greeted them. After chatting with Heidi for a couple of hours, the men said they had to leave in order to get home before dark. As they donned their rucksacks and prepared to leave the hut, they noticed the sky had grown leaden and that heavy snowflakes were already falling.*

"*Just then the shortwave radio in the hut crackled a foul weather warning, and they realized that they would be in grave danger if they tried to climb down the dark, slippery trail. Heidi urged them to spend the night with her in the hut. They agreed hesitantly, knowing how their father would worry when they did not return that night. 'Father has taught us to respect the mountain,' said Joshua. 'He will understand.'*

"After a hearty dinner of vegetable and beef soup, pumpernickel bread, and strong Swiss cheese, Heidi secured the shutters and door to the Hutte and began preparing for bed."

At this point in the fantasy story I looked out the window to see the towering clouds slowly drifting up the Matterhorn toward the summit, exposing the firm base. Was the mountain flirting with me?

"Heidi lifted her skirts," I whispered, telling my own Josh to look at the mountain while I continued. He lay there transfixed in my arms, as peaceful as a child. I continued.

"The brothers stood shyly by while watching Heidi pull her skirts over her head to expose her white lace panties and her large breasts straining against her cotton camisole. 'I do not sleep in clothes,' she said matter-of-factly. Then she turned her back, flung off her panties and camisole, and crawled beneath the pile of blankets on the floor. With her golden head cradled in her arms, she looked invitingly at the brothers and allowed the tops of her breasts to emerge from the covers. 'I love mountains,' she said. 'Have you ever thought how women have mountains on their chests and men have mountains in their pants?' Both Hans and Joshua had enormous erections which they did not bother to hide. Heidi smiled invitingly as they stripped naked and joined her in her nest."

Now the clouds outside our window were ascending smoothly to obscure the peak while three-quarters of the Matterhorn's face shone like a jewel in the setting sun. My Josh, whose face was nuzzled deep into my right breast, lifted his head to catch the view. I felt his large erect cock pressing into my thigh and I swiftly guided him on top of me. We began to make love.

"Tell me what you see," he said, pumping slowly into my depths.

"I see Hans and Joshua each sucking a snowy tit. Heidi has grasped each man's cock and is gently squeezing their tips, smoothing the drops of pre-ejaculation fluid over them. When Hans moves his mouth to her mound, Joshua sticks his cock in her mouth. She takes it deep into her throat while Hans's tongue drives deep into her core."

Our pace quickened and as we pressed together, I could feel his heart pounding wildly, matching the rhythm of my own. "Tell me more," urged my Joshua as we rolled over still united, with me on top.

"Joshua and Heidi came simultaneously, Joshua's cock throbbing in her throat, Heidi's strong thighs clenching and unclenching spasmodically. 'Fuck me, Hans!' she cried, and Hans obeyed, thrusting his cock deep inside her while Joshua glued his lips to hers. They performed this way for a long time. Finally, Hans withdrew his cock and let his brother take his place atop the thrashing girl. 'Matterhorn,' she screamed."

Outside our window, all but the very peak of the mountain had come into view. The huge base stood majestically, shining like a saber, jabbing its razor teeth into the heavens. Josh and I were both spellbound by the sight. I fucked my lover slowly, my breasts in his hands.

"Heidi was clawing Joshua's back, her body bathed in sweat. Hans knelt beside them and placed his cock in her mouth," I whispered. Immediately I pulled away and turned around so I could suck my Josh while

his tongue licked my clit. Josh's cock throbbed the one special beat that signaled that he was about to come. Just then the final cloud ascended, revealing the splendid summit, and I drew back my head. Josh's semen splashed my face.

"They sucked and fucked all night, darling, just like us."

During our trip throughout Switzerland we occasionally met a woman or girl named Heidi. This would always bring a secret smile to our faces. When we returned to the "States" I bought a beautifully bound version of the classic fairy tale *Heidi* for Josh's Christmas stocking.

What If Your Man Gets Too Excited?

Believe it or not, that could happen. My close friend, Connie, who had religiously practiced everything in the first four chapters of this book, called me quite alarmed one morning.

"I tried it," she cried. "I did everything you suggested. Practiced for weeks with my tape recorder, talked dirty to the Dial-A-Prayer recording, even screwed up the courage to bring my gorgeous neighbor into his fantasy story. Well, he got so excited that one-quarter of the way into my first tale he finally pleaded, *'Oh, shut up and suck my cock!'* "

What does this mean? Perhaps you are going too far and too fast. If you go back and examine those magic moments, you'll be able to develop a sense of timing that fits your man. If he gets too excited too soon, slow it down; you'll be able to finish the story eventually. Try telling him the same fantasy story several times until he knows it well and knows exactly what to expect. Let him learn *your* rhythm. Then, just when he seems to fall into a comfortable pattern, speed up to delight him.

Marking That Magic Moment

During your first attempt, did you reach a critical point during your story when your man quickly escalated from lukewarm, to rapid boil, to fiery inferno? Look for clues between those stages to find the triggers that set him off. Was it the setting, something you did or said, your costume? Or did a particular episode in the story launch him from one state to the next? The morning after, treat yourself to an instant replay of the action, looking for both obvious and subtle clues. For example, did his cock twitch madly when you said, "Take a peek at my asshole"? Once you detect the clues, you can weave them into your subsequent stories, embellishing them or timing them for precisely the right effect.

Blowing Your Man's Mind Without Lifting a Finger

Years ago, Pavlov demonstrated that if you ring a bell for a dog and then give it food, the dog will gradually become conditioned to the ringing of the bell, until finally, if you ring a bell, the dog will salivate in anticipation of being fed.

Wouldn't you like to reach the point where you could put together a short string of words or images that would rocket your man to the point of orgasm without your even lifting a finger? You can if you are a good observer. Watch for bell ringing reactions to certain words, gestures, costumes, and sounds in order to invent a magic formula that will light the booster rocket of even a tired man intent on reading the evening paper. Imagine being able for you to walk up to your man while wearing nothing but a trenchcoat, whisper "Acapulco" in his ear, and have him chase you around the room!

Sooner or Later I'm Gonna Getcha!

Have you gotten to a critical point in your fantasy storytelling, but your man's initial response has been less (or more) than you expected? Professional salespeople have mastered the art and science of persuasion which is always well-timed and demonstrates patient persistence. And you can learn a lot about mastering your man by putting yourself on the receiving end of a good sales pitch. Take your pick: approach your local Mercedes dealer, or visit the most expensive dress salon in town (naturally you want to be dressed to kill anyway). Encourage the salesperson to persuade you, and *study their timing*. You'll notice that:

- They assume you are going to buy.
- Whether it's a car or a dress, they let you try it out (or on).
- They let you slowly get the feel of the new situation.
- Then, they tell you how great it looks on you or you look in it.
- And if they don't make a sale, do they leave you high and dry? No. They give you time to think it over, urging you to come back. The door is always open. With a friendly gesture and a smile, they

wave you off. But notice the look in their eyes. They know you'll be back, if not tomorrow, maybe next week.

Persistence Pays

What happens when you have spent hours weaving delicious tales of fantasy for your lover and he still doesn't respond with the enthusiasm you hope for? Persistence pays, so don't give up the ship. Besides, you may literally be whispers away from the magic formula that sets his pulse racing. Once you discover that magic formula you will reach the point where you can stimulate your lover with a simple glance, a soft word, or a gentle gesture. Consider how Aline's persistence paid off.

"I spent several weeks practicing until I was sure I could deliver a ten-megaton fantasy story that would detonate his desire. But I was surprised to discover that although he reveled in the story and urged me to keep going, he was having so much trouble reaching his climax.

"I began to feel disheartened. What was wrong? My costume was perfect—a beige camisole with no panties. I used all the right words, and I had the Eagles' 'Hotel California' pulsating from my stereo speakers. Still, something seemed to be missing. Then at one point I spotted the clue. He groaned and said, 'I wish we were under a waterfall.'

"Niagara Falls! His favorite romantic setting! Since a trip was out of the question at the moment, I reached into my treasure chest for the waterfall posters I had collected. His favorite one showed a Hawaiian girl offering her bare breasts to a cascading jungle stream. I quickly taped up six posters around my waterbed.

" 'Lie back and relax,' I whispered as I changed

records, replacing the Eagles with a recording of jungle sounds. 'Pretend we've just checked into a swank hotel at Niagara Falls.' Earlier I had taken a handsome full-color brochure advertising just such a place. So I handed it to him, urging him to read it, while I settled back on the bed with my hand under his balls. I had typed my own words on plain paper and glued them over the advertising copy:

"Niagara is a place for all seasons—winter, summer, spring, and fall all abound in exciting holiday experiences, including the best blowjobs in the world.

"At the Notell Motel—a warm haven of gracious accommodations complete with mirrored ceilings and small waterfalls in each Honeymoon Suite—you will be transported to a tropical dreamland. Our facilities include waterbeds, a computerized matching service for couples interested in group sex, and videotape equipment you can use to record your best sex ever. Between November 15 and April 15 our Special Off-Season rates will make your tour of Swingers' Paradise easily affordable. Plan your trip to fantasyland today!"

"My boyfriend's penis got very hard, so I gave him his favorite blowjob, firmly massaging his balls while I sucked hard on the head of his penis with an ice cube in my mouth. (All I have to do when we're out to dinner is pull an ice cube out of my glass and suck it thoughtfully, and he scrambles out of his chair to whisk me home. More than one maître d' has had to chase him with the check!)"

EXERCISE 6

Memorizing Those Magic Moments

Jot down the appropriate words, phrases, gestures, sounds, smells, and so forth into a chant that will ignite blast-off! For example:

- He starts to get hard when I ________________.
- He reaches full erection when I ______________.
- His cock begins to throb when I ______________.
- His testicles move forward when I ____________.
- He begins to make mad passionate love when I ____.
- __________ starts his cock twitching.
- __________ turns his cock into pre-orgasm steel.
- He explodes in a spine-shattering climax when I ____________________ and ____________________.
- Then, I can rekindle his excitement again and again by ____ ____.

LESSON 6

Hit Show!

After several fantasy story sessions, Liz, an exquisite-looking television reporter who inhabited many male viewers' fantasies, noticed that her lover's response to her newly developed sexual assertiveness was waning. Even her pink satin underwear seemed to have lost its electric effect. What was wrong? Knowing Paul used to be a Freedom Rider in the 60's, Liz wondered whether her normally mild-mannered, even-tempered lover harbored secret fantasies of becoming a revolutionary leader. Since he often spoke passionately about the plight of black South African miners, Liz decided to pluck some material from the eleven o'clock news. Here's what she told Paul:

"Tonight there was a mining accident in Johannesburg. Many men died. But if you had been there, you would have saved them.

"You know, I sometimes picture you naked to the waist, your muscles rippling in the sun and bulging as you swing your huge hammer against the rock. Imagine the terror in your men's eyes when the roof of the mine began crumbling! And imagine their respect when you singlehandedly shoved up the ceiling with a beam.

"After you saved their lives, you led your men out of the mine and went straight to the foreman's cabin. 'Until working conditions are safe, we will never work in the mines again,' you said sternly. Just then a long, navy blue Mercedes limousine pulled up and out stepped Angelica, the beautiful daughter of the owner of the mine. Seeing your beautiful body glistening with sweat, and noticing the definitions of your bulging muscles, she discreetly called you aside. 'Meet me here at midnight,' she whispered, not daring to look into your smoldering black eyes. Although you knew you could be killed for touching the boss's daughter, you were enthralled with her cool beauty.

"Later that evening you met her. She talked with you for a while about working conditions in the mine, then promised to influence her father into making some important changes. As you walked her back to her car she tripped on a rock and fell straight into your arms. You knew you should let her go, but your hungry mouth found her ruby lips and you poured forth with such passionate kisses that she pulled away from you. 'Not here, in the car,' she whispered, and the two of you ran to her waiting limo.

"Settled into the back seat, she pulled up her white linen frock to reveal a pair of shapely legs and a pair of

white lace panties covering her mound. 'Just eat me, I'm still a virgin,' she whispered. And without any more encouragement, you dove between her legs, devouring her sweet pussy until finally you took out your cock and brought yourself relief.

"Within a few days she had kept her word: safer conditions were promised and acted upon, and your men went back to work. Oh, I love fucking a hero. I love your beautiful ass and cock!"

Liz's man loves being her hero in bed. Each story she spins has him triumphing over the forces of oppression and making every woman who sees him get moist between her legs. Paul gets especially excited when Liz dreams that he's won the Nobel Peace Prize.

Liz and Paul got married last year and moved to the suburbs where they look forward to having their first child. Now in the last month of her pregnancy, Liz can no longer have intercourse, but she keeps her man faithful to her bed and body by mining material for ever more potent fantasies.

Clues That Signal a Need to Advance

Like clever Liz, you need to scan your man's reactions for hints that he needs something a bit more daring from you. As your man nibbles away at your little victory garden of eden, he will be bound to fall into two predictable patterns:

1. He'll begin to find plain carrots routine, or
2. He'll savor some spicier sources.

The key to satisfying the gourmet palate? Love and romance. Every man and woman wants to feel loved and special, longing to evoke a mature, sensitive response from his or her partner. When you show your man that you can turn even the simplest dish into an exotic feast, you'll find him relishing both sex and romance. Costumes, props, and settings spice up a relationship, and romantic touches always add zest. When you sail your cargo ship into port, your man will be waving the banner of lust!

Do you worry that you're not the creative, artistic type? With all the sexy magazines and professional advertisements at your fingertips, you'll quickly become an artist between the sheets.

Keeping Your Budding Romance from Losing Its Bloom

There's not a man alive that cannot be dazzled. Though only *you* can know what will dazzle your own man, you might experiment with these tried and tested ideas.

- Name a star for him. Did you know you really can have a single star registered for your man? (Princess Diana received one as a wedding gift.) The address is listed in the Whole Fantasy Catalogue at the back of this book.
- Write your fantasy love message across the skies by hiring a skywriting plane to celebrate a special moment. Just imagine his shock and pride when he looks up from his box seats at the next football game and his rowdy friends slap him on the back, saying, "What a woman you've got, Hank!"
- Send him flowers. While the long-stemmed red rose remains the ultimate symbol of affection, you might create a wildflower bouquet or send a holly wreath on the Fourth of July.

- Select from the countless gorgeous, often blank, greeting cards for your surprise messages to your man—especially when he's out of town on business.
- Charter a yacht, complete with discreet captain and crew for a weekend or weeklong sail.
- Place an interior ad on the bus he rides to work. A big spender might even rent a billboard.
- Hire a limousine for the evening and pick him up at his office.
- Find out where you can take a ride in a horse-drawn carriage. Anything from hansom cab to snow sleigh will do depending on the weather.
- Have a love song written and recorded for him, perhaps with a hidden fantasy message. Check the Whole Fantasy Catalogue for the address.
- Write special fortunes which a baker can put inside Chinese fortune cookies.
- Whip up a love potion.
- Take him to an out-of-the-way ballroom for some cheek-to-cheek dancing.
- Give him a handsome coupon booklet for thirty personal treats ranging from a massage by you to a blowjob in heavy traffic.
- Give him a bath, read him erotic poems, towel him dry, powder him, and then take him to bed.
- Give him useful gifts like tools, a wheelbarrow, or sheepskin car seatcovers—all with his fantasy in mind.

Paste-up Material

- Obtain a nice photo album and some copies of *Penthouse* and *Playgirl* magazines. Paste up a tender or sexy photograph of your man among two women making love. Or tape his face over a well-hung male model. Can you think up clever captions? One inventive vixen took a *Playgirl* calendar and redesigned it with her man's head on the twelve different hunks' bodies! On the first day of each month she turns a page and launches into a brand new tale starring her own man-of-the-month.
- Paste a photo of your face onto a sexy star's poster and then tack it onto the back of your bedroom door. Or if you're in a funny mood, graft your face onto the body of his favorite animal.
- Ransack his Sexual Fantasy Inventory for images that excite him! Put him in the driver's seat of a white Excalibur; slip your naked body into a trout stream; or tape the two of you onto the beach at Waikiki.
- Ask him to help you tailor a photo fantasies scrapbook, each of you taking turns. When he adds a big-breasted bombshell to the left-hand page, you put a well-endowed young stud on the right-hand page, producing a nice rhythm between his fantasies and your own. This game can help him begin to unlock your Pandora's box and set him on the path toward whispering in *your* ear.

"Parker takes my fantasy scrapbook on business trips," says Martha. "Instead of hitting the bars at night, he works on it, knowing I'm propped up in bed with a glass of sherry figuring out ways to blow his mind when he gets home."

Costumes

Don't save costumes for Halloween or for a neighbor's costume party. If you are going to create a lion tamer fantasy story, then get yourself dolled up as a pussycat or lady liontamer, complete with boots and whip. Dress up in your man's clothes, particularly his underwear; many men get stimulated seeing their lover in a favorite bulky bathrobe or old flannel shirt. Unusual combinations like these often turn the trick:

- Spike-heeled shoes with a pair of running shorts. Cowboy boots with a lacy camisole.
- One friend wraps herself in a ticker tape for her boyfriend, the stock market *maven*.
- Another friend's authentic-looking nun's habit reinforces her man's wildest fantasy.
- Decorate your new G-string with playful, unusual, items such as: eagle feathers, jingle bells, brightly colored ribbons. I know a woman who hangs Christmas balls from her brassiere and weaves silver tinsel in her hair.
- My lover's favorite costume on me is a black garter belt, genuine silk stockings, a black lacy scoop-front bra, stiletto-heeled shoes, and a "Pick Maine Potatoes" hat jauntily perched on top of my head.
- Since one man's Tinker Bell may be another's Gypsy Rose Lee, keep trying different accessories until you find the most effective ones.
- Don't overlook the obvious. A nurse's boyfriend seemed turned off by all her experiments—a New

York Yankees warm-up jacket, a pair of green satin harem pants, and a surgeon's scrub suit. Then one day they made love before she had a chance to change out of her nurse's uniform, and that drove him wild.

- If he has a foot fetish, figure out *exactly* what types of shoes turn him on.
- What about false fingernails or eyelashes, fresh flowers in your hair, or a washable butterfly tattoo decal on your inner thigh? Some women actually visit tattoo parlors for small personalized tattoos, not just a heart with their name in the center, but images that really excite their men, such as small hummingbirds perched about their Venus mounds.

After two or three months into my love affair with Ryan, I handed him a felt-tip pen one evening after I had worn a first communion dress (complete with patent leather shoes), and asked him to propose the next fantasy costume by writing it on my thigh. He wrote his name. Undaunted. I soon chose a fantasy story tailored for his fortieth birthday.

After persuading a couple of our closest friends, Meggy and Dieter, to dress as Ryan frequently does—in chino trousers, blue oxford shirt, striped tie, and navy blue V-neck sweaters, we all drove with Ryan to our favorite Provincetown restaurant with trenchcoats covering our costumes. When we finally exposed ourselves to Ryan, he howled and then gave me a knowing wink. We made beautiful love that night. And before we fell asleep, he reached for a pen and wrote "ice cream cone" on my belly. Ice cream cone? Why not? Which leads us to the use of props.

Props

When most women think of sexual props, they naturally picture dildoes, vibrators, french ticklers, and the like. Though you'll want to include such items in your toolbox, don't forget candles, food, feathers, bells, toys, hobby accessories, furniture, and *objets d'art*.

Amanda told me the following about her lover's favorite fantasy story, in which she plays the queen to Evan's slave.

"I bought a gaudy rhinestone tiara and a magician's wand to which I fastened a sequined gold star. After commanding my slave to put the black satin sheets on the bed, I ordered chocolate Häagen Dazs ice cream. While I tickled my pussy with my scepter, I told my slave to spoon ice cream into my mouth, and onto my belly and breasts. He liked the part where he got to lick up the mess.

"When I finally gave him permission to masturbate himself, I stopped him in midstroke, sternly admonishing him not to come before I do. In this fantasy we never touch each other, just play with ourselves.

"I realized how important the crown was one evening when, as I was about to come, my tiara fell to the pillow and Evan paused. 'Your crown, my queen!' he cried out. His penis went limp. But the minute I crowned myself again, he stood to attention. And soon we climaxed simultaneously."

In the Whole Fantasy Catalogue you'll find a list of sources for out-of-this-world props such as:

- Body glitter
- Edible body paints
- Body Gello—wet, slippery and wild
- Fragrant body oils in the most erotic flavors

- Where to learn how to make erotic foods such as chopped liver molded into a penis shape, complete with "matzoh balls"
- Sexy birthday cakes
- Edible underpants
- Inflatable dolls for the safest *ménage à trois*

Lara, a sensational raven-haired dancer, knew that her lover liked to watch her trim her pussy hair (something necessary for her profession). And she knew that in his fantasy he would like for him to shave her pussy clean.

Over a three-month period, each time Lara told her man a fantasy story, she kept his zippered-up shaving kit nearby on the night table. Then one night Lara installed a hot lather machine next to the now-opened shaving kit and urged her lover to play barber. Shaving her clean gave both of them immeasurable joy. Once shaven, Lara had to wait several weeks for enough growth in order to repeat the performance. During that time the shaving kit remained securely closed on the night table, but her lover never tired of rubbing hot lather between her legs.

When it dawned on Lara that *he* might enjoy being shaved, she found him terrifically turned on by the idea. To her erotic scrapbook she added a color Polaroid shot of his erection, which seemed especially big against the white backdrop of his shaven groin.

Photography

Talk about instant gratification! Every serious fantasy story-teller should own a good camera! Nothing is more rewarding or more stimulating than instant photography. The quality of the prints has increased, while the prices have fallen into any woman's reach. Does your man want to photograph his very own centerfold?

Before the onset of instant photography and the liberalization of many film developers' policies, many a frustrated male built his own darkroom in order to satisfy his desire to photograph a naked woman.

Nowadays most men have taken sexually revealing photographs. Who poses for them? Housewives and girls next door like you and I—P.T.A. presidents, congresswomen, and the editors of small town newspapers. So why not model for your man? If he's going to masturbate to any woman's photograph, let it be yours. A friend recently showed me a photograph of herself seven months pregnant, a satin sheet seductively drawn between her legs to discover her swollen belly, her full, ripe breasts annointed with baby oil, and her caressing a pearly necklace. Mona Lisa in heat! It is one of the most beautiful photographs I have ever seen. She employs it at the tenderest moments. And men often like to join in the photograph; there are many cameras which have delayed exposure buttons.

If you wish to be more daring, and your man is not the jealous type, you can portray your lusty beauty best for a professional photographer.

Go all the way if you can afford it. Hire a fashion photographer; have your makeup and hair done by professionals. And invite your man to view the sitting. Those pictures of you with the kids at the beach are nice for his office wall, but a professionally lighted, expertly finished photo of his one and only belongs in the top drawer of his desk. When the photographer starts snapping, think about your man making love to you, not in the abstract, but in reality. Imagine his hand running under your dress, his fingers finding their way beneath your panties. Your smoldering appeal will thereby be caught by the camera. On the back of the photo, where no one will see it, write a few key fantasy words.

When you present him with the finished product, tell him what you were thinking when the shutter snapped.

A few months after you've given him the photograph, call him at the office and suggest he remove the photo from the frame and read what's on the back to you over the phone.

Video

What better Christmas present than a home recording set, complete with camera? Endless hours of X-rated fun await the daring "Cecilia B. De Mille." If you have a close friend to help you out, you can record video fantasies while you and your man are apart, or you can tape or rent X-rated films, splicing them into your own home movies.

Don't limit your filming sessions to your bedroom. Walk around the house. Or better yet, go to the most beautiful setting in town, filming footage of the two of you playing in the surf, picnicking in a flower-filled meadow, playing tennis, or making love in a pasture full of cows. Be mischievous, open, and free. If you are caressing yourself on a bed of rose petals, have a cassette recorder playing classical background music.

My friend Adrianna asked me to film her walking along the beach near my home. She wore a transparent, white gauze dress with nothing underneath. As she walked, the wind blew, alternately exposing and outlining her body. The next scene featured Adrianna rising out of the ocean topless. Her well-oiled body shone in the sunlight, yet the cold Atlantic made her large nipples as hard as pebbles. Then Adrianna simply stood there, eyes wandering, smiling to herself, the sound of the crashing surf and the cries of seagulls supplying musical accompaniment. The final footage showed Adrianna lying completely naked on the bare sand, her left hand stroking herself from breast to thigh. We closed with a closeup of her lovely face.

This was her wedding gift to her man, Diego. Now, several years later, their marriage is rock-solid. Adrianna, European born and raised, advised me to tell my readers never to let the romance slip from a relationship. "It's the hardest job a woman has to do," she says. "Men stay faithful to an attentive, inventive woman. We must make our men feel special." Frankly, ladies, if you don't consider your man special enough to go to a little (or to a lot of) trouble, chances are you're with the wrong man.

If you have a video recorder, you can produce the X-rated "Tonight Show." For example:

1. You could tape yourself delivering a newscast, "Sex in the News," during which you get so excited that you end up making love to the camera.

2. You and a friend could interview each other, playing host and guest star. The host can ask penetrating questions that will help your man begin *his* Sexual Fantasy Inventory of *you,* asking questions like, "What makes you come the quickest?"

3. You and your man can play "60 Minutes" as interviewer and elusive quarry. One woman told me this was the only way she could finally get her electronics-hobbyist spouse to open up enough for her to unlock his fantasy life.

Publicity

Once you're a world-class fantasy story-teller, you'll want to use a little publicity. Learn from Madison Avenue, or, to paraphrase Dorothy Sayers, "Sex must advertise."

1. When writing or tape-recording fantasies, develop your own special logo, such as two tree frogs making love. Imprint your lips on labels, envelopes, and stationery. Your logo might become the stimulus that rings your man's bell.
2. Put your most distinctive portable prop in his briefcase. It might raise his temperature a few degrees in the middle of a business meeting, but your man will want to wrap up the deal quickly and race into your arms. Of course, you must be absolutely sure your prop will not pop out during an important meeting and cause embarrassment.
3. If you and your man are apart, send a postcard with a few key words from a recent fantasy story along with your logo.
4. Leave the introduction to your next fantasy story on his telephone answering machine. Say something like, "The next time we make love I'm going to pretend that you just pitched a no-hitter, and then I'm going to go after one of your balls."

Computer Softpornware

Is your man hooked on spending his evenings staring at a video display terminal, tapping like a blindman on his keyboard, inserting his floppy disks in his tape drive? Well, he's about to fall madly in love, except he doesn't know it yet. Buy him a computerized dirty game! No I'm not kidding; computer softpornware can fill even the most incurable computer jockey's fantasy stocking. Next time he turns away and heads for his personal computer, pull up a chair and introduce him to the softest ware in town.

Betty Ferrarini, author of *Confessions of an Infomaniac,* rented a computer terminal even though she had no programming experience, and used *The Source's* electronic bulletin board to meet hundreds of eligible (and wealthy) men. With inexpensive machines and user-friendly software, any woman can go from technophobiac one day, to infomaniac the next.

LESSON 7

Earning Your X-Rating

If you're like most women, you entered fantasyland not just for your own erotic stimulation, but to help you form a deep, lasting, and unique bond with your man. You crave commitment. Now, having convinced him how important he is to you, you may feel compelled to turn up the heat.

Fantasy stories can demand progression from a first giggly high, to a technicolor hallucination, and finally to multidimensional lust. Although you may feel you've done enough to fascinate your man for life, you will want to look closely for signs that his fantasy dosage needs a little boost. Does he yawn when you strip to your orange panties with the jack-o-lantern face? Has he begun to doze off in the middle of your formerly successful yarn about the cheerleader and the basketball center? Well, it may be time to visit the fantasy medicine chest for something a little stronger.

Strong Medicine

When one flirts with excitement, fear, and danger, one's appetite increases, raising the threshold at which our adrenaline flows. At first we may sit on the edge of our seats as we watch climbers on television conquer Mt. Everest, but we soon need something more daring—an unequipped "spiderman" scaling the World Trade Center. Though Gunther Gebel-Williams once excited us in his cage of raging tigers, we eventually hunger to see him stick his head in a cat's mouth. And so it happens with sex. While thoughts of certain forms of more exotic sex may not initially be appealing, we fantasy people often find ourselves increasingly open to temptation.

Most women find it easier to approach kinkier sex aurally. Many never go further than to weave it into their fantasy stories, while others turn their talk into action.

As your man becomes more familiar and comfortable with your nurturing of his fantasy world, he may willingly reveal, or you may uncover, certain preferences you may have previously considered kinky. Whether or not you choose to exploit such preferences verbally or physically depends on your own particular upbringing and set of mores, though, you'll probably find yourself more than mildly interested.

A word of caution: dangerous sexual preferences such as rape, beating, or playing with weapons are *never* recommended, nor should they be brought into fantasy stories. Anything that can be harmful to a person's physical body or psyche is strongly discouraged. Stay away from it!

Remember, men fantasize about a woman who accepts all forms of healthy sexuality. As you become more advanced in your fantasy story-telling you may find that so-called "forbidden" sex is indeed the sexiest sex of all for your man and for you.

What makes kinky sex so attractive? It's the forbidden fruit, the sinful apple dangling from the tree of sexual knowledge, which, once bitten, influences our tastes forever. For fantasy ladies who have shrugged off the chains of convention, forbidden sex can be an ultra-erotic delight. Be careful. Start gradually by observing his responses. For example, if you tell him that you are making love to him while he is wearing satin panties, and he immediately becomes more aroused, continue. But if you tell him that you are darting your tongue up and down his cock while his sister watches, and he loses his crection, stop.

Picking Your First Apple

Almost all of us ease into forbidden sex gradually. The following letter sent to me by a Baptist preacher's wife from Augusta, Georgia, illustrates my point:

"A friend talked me into writing to you because she thought my experience might help a lot of ladies like her. First, I want to tell you a little about me and the Reverend Mr. Black. We've been married for thirty-four years and have always enjoyed straight sex. Our three children are grown and gone now, all happily married.

"Well, when the kids moved away, I had no one to mother, and the Reverend Mr. Black began to turn

into 'my baby.' It's true. Every Saturday night, along about nine o'clock, the Reverend will say to me, 'Momma, how's about telling your baby a beddy-bye story?'

"Well, he's still a very attractive man, and lots of the ladies, especially the widows, just faint when he preaches hellfire and brimstone. Sometimes I think they'd sell their souls to the devil to be in my place. Don't get me wrong, he's a righteous man, but he's always said, 'Anything goes, behind closed doors.'

"When he's all tense after rehearsing the next day's sermon, he takes a hot bath while I fetch our shotguns. When he comes into the bedroom, which is decorated all pink and frilly, I say, 'Come to Bonnie, Clyde,' and then I say, 'Did you see the look on that teller's face when you told him you were collecting alms for the poor?' Remember driving through the next town? A young, sweet-faced girl was standing on the corner looking sad, so you stopped the car so I could roll down the window and hand her a wad of twenty-dollar bills. Big tears rolled down her cheeks and she asked if she could come with us. God, wasn't it fun sailing down the country roads in our big shiny convertible, the wind blowing my hair, my hand squeezing her firm, young leg? When she saw our guns we told her we were Bonnie and Clyde, and her eyes got big and she squirmed in her seat. I touched her panties. 'She's wet, Clyde,' I said, and you rolled your big cigar in your mouth, winking and smiling wickedly. 'Oh, Momma!' you said.

"We went straight to the next motel, and once we were inside I gave her a good hot bath, rubbing her all over with the slippery soap, while you were out for roast beef sandwiches and a bottle of Jack Daniels. We partied a bit with her sitting cross-legged and naked in the bed, your big old .30-.30 cradled in her

arms. She fondled the handcarved stock and rubbed her cheek against the barrel. After I stripped you, she whispered, 'I'm a virgin,' which made your rod get long and hard. 'That's okay, honey,' I said, 'Mr. Black likes all our ladyholes, dontcha, Daddy?' I took my shotgun and ran it between her legs until it was moist and glistening. Then I rolled her over, greased up her ass with baby oil, and you slid into her from the rear while I rubbed the wet gun between my legs. 'Fuck her ass, Daddy!' I screamed, and you pump until we both come.

"The next day my husband delivers his best sermon ever."

Hmmm. Imagine, a preacher's wife down South! What does such a fantasy mean? Are the Reverend and Mrs. Black perverted? Not at all. Mr. Black spends his life as a caregiver, privy to the deepest, darkest secrets of his flock. Mrs. Black knows how to relieve the tension that takes hold of a genuinely compassionate man. Playing Robin Hood, seducing a young virgin without despoiling her—being able to work out the pressures of his profession—does no harm at all. Notice that he calls his wife "Momma"? *Momma* permits his fantasy. Snuggled safely in the loving environment of their boudoir, "Momma" exorcises the Devil without practicing what she preaches.

A famous film director with more than one Oscar on his mantel confided to me, "I still have trouble imagining my mother having sex with my father. I tell my friends that she had sex three times in her life: when she conceived me and my two sisters."

This is no joke. Some men suffer extreme anxiety imagining their mother's sexuality. What a potent taboo! What would mommy say if she knew her dimpled, darling son fantasized about or practiced *anal* sex? Shame! Or worse, what if Sonny secretly longed to dress up in mommy's clothes! Or yearned to host an orgy in Macy's window during the Christmas rush? Double shame! Since he's thrust these secret fantasies deep inside his brain and has wasted enormous energy keeping them buried, imagine the sexual power you can tap when you give permission for him to face them, possibly even revel in them. That brings us back to the notion that:

When You're Good You're Great, but When You're Bad You're Better!

When Loretta, a dynamic marketing executive with a large computer software developer, had to address a major sales meeting, she invited her boyfriend Sean to attend. Sean openly admitted to Loretta's being an imaginative lover, a solid friend, a terrific professional success, not to mention a fine gardener and excellent cook. To top it off, she's a master fantasy storyteller. Sean told her, "You're so naughty, Loretta! If your mother ever heard what comes out of your beautiful mouth, she'd wash it out with soap." Well, what if *his* mother ever heard what Loretta says to Sean? Let's eavesdrop!

"The last time we made love I had this funny feeling that you wanted to slide your cock into my asshole. I got so excited thinking about it that I got off just picturing such a scene while we made regular love.

"First, I imagined you were licking my pussy when suddenly your gentle tongue searched for and found my other hole. The tingling sensation was unlike anything I had ever known. Soon you were exploring me with your tongue until I thought I would die with pleasure. Slowly you slid your finger in. I felt like a

virgin again, making it with you for the first time. As I sighed and moaned, begging for your cock, you pushed the whole shaft in. I began to wriggle around on your cock. Then suddenly you pulled out and handed me a warm, soapy washcloth.

"After I bathed you carefully, I began to lick your balls. And soon my tongue found its way to your ass. At first you jerked away, saying that it tickled, but soon I found the magic spot and began to dart my tongue all around. When you were well-lubricated, I slid one finger into your opening. You squealed in delight. So I slid another finger in, and then another, until finally I got up enough courage to strap on a big rubbery dildo and slide it fully inside you. 'You're a virgin, too,' I whispered, and you begged me not to stop, until finally you shot out a huge load of semen."

What clue did Loretta use to help lead her to Sean's deeply hidden fantasy? Well, Sean had always claimed that he was anal compulsive, tight-assed in business and tennis. But the key turned out to be the fact that, despite their wide experience with other lovers before they met, in the category of anal sex, Sean and Loretta really *were* virgins and could obtain the secret pleasure of deflowering each other.

Group Sex While the Whole World Watches

Although group sex infuses many fantasies, it rarely involves more than four people. Although one may think of group sex as wild and wicked, one tends to want to control it in order to feel safe. Nowhere does sexual competition grow more fierce than among two men and two women; men are particularly anxious about their performance. Often when a man fantasizes about group sex he hopes his woman will give him permission without feeling threatened; he wants his woman to know that he loves her best and will bring back to her new tricks and dreams. An open, sophisticated man may confide his secret desire to participate in an orgy, but when he actually gets the chance, he may shyly back away if he fears losing his own partner's respect and faithfulness. Of special significance, too, is the possibility of homosexual contact during group sex, even if only accidental.

Talk about taboos! Obviously, aural group sex can offer the rewards of such encounters without risk. This next fantasy story shows how one woman fulfilled her lover's fantasies:

"You have such a perfect body, you could be a male stripper," Daphne purred to her lover John, a construction worker with hard muscles and a deep tan. "You'd be a world champion! Macy's would hire you to perform in their window. Wouldn't it be lovely if this year's Macy's Christmas display theme was 'Superstud,' with you the star attraction! You'd wear a Santa Claus suit. Your friend Jeff would play a satyr instead of a reindeer, and two lady gymnasts would be Santa's elves.

"Can't you see the big four-poster bed and the girls in their green and red nighties fondling each other on an old Christmas quilt? Are their lips on each other's nipples, their fingers brushing their cunts? Bruce Springsteen is singing a rocking 'Santa Claus Is Coming to Town' over the loud speakers, and a large crowd of shoppers is shouldering to see the display.

"When midnight approaches, Jeff bounds upon the bed, frightening the girls with his hairy chest and goatskin leotard. Their eyes grow round and their hands fly to their mouths. When Jeff kneels between them and places his hands on their slick cunts, you

bow to the audience, then leap onto the bed. The girls are getting aroused, moaning softly, almost whimpering. But they can't take their eyes off you as you dance a gentle and sensuous strip-tease. Off flies your hat and boots, your red shirt and pants, until soon you have nothing on but a transparent pair of jockey shorts with mistletoe on the crotch.

"Glancing at the audience, you see that a large-breasted woman has unbuttoned her coat despite the cold weather outside and is blowing you kisses. Bruce Springsteen's voice grows husky and the music grows louder. Jeff has released his hard cock from the goatskin and strips the girls while massaging their cheeks, tits, and cunts with its tip. They squeal when you remove your shorts. Your huge cock dwarfs even Jeff's. And the lady in the audience has taken off all her clothes, letting several men pet and caress her without ever taking her eyes off your *cock.*

"While Jeff puts his own cock in the mouth of the blond elf, you pull the dark-haired one to her feet and begin to dance. Jeff pumps himself into his elf's mouth, and the men outside lift their own naked lady over their heads, taking turns licking her cunt. You dance faster and faster, your partner's tits bounce wildly, and Jeff comes in great thundering bursts all over his own lover's breasts. Spent, he curls up on the quilt. But his ladyfriend joins you and your partner in the dance. Outside, the naked lady has begun to suck off each man in the audience, her eyes still glued to your swinging cock.

"Unable to restrain herself, the blond elf climbs up your body and impales herself, while the brunette stands behind you, rubbing her tits on your back and biting your neck. Soon she too climbs up, and you dance wildly with both women clinging to you. You're

so strong, and so manly. The woman in the audience presses her pussy to the window and you pull out of your partner and splatter come all over the window separating you from the woman outside. You laugh madly when you finally recognize that it's me."

A tamer version of an exhibitionist fantasy that also fulfills the secret desire of getting caught comes from a young editor I met recently at a party in Cambridge. When he heard about *Whisper in His Ear*, this calm, cool, slightly arrogant intellectual took me aside to confide a fantasy that his female friend, an artist from New York, had created for him just the weekend before:

"I had to meet with an author in Maine, on Saturday. So I took Autumn along, hoping I could wind up business quickly and drive up into the White Mountains. By two o'clock, we were weaving my little Lotus up the winding mountain roads. What had dawned as a crisp fall day soon turned chill and wintry, with November's first snowflakes obscuring the view of the mountains.

"The huge old Mt. Washington Hotel was closed for the season, so we checked into the motor lodge across the highway. It was a new place with modern rooms, views of snowcapped peaks, and a luxurious indoor pool, sauna, and Jacuzzi.

" 'Let's play in the snow,' Autumn suggested. So we drove up to the cog railway, where two inches of fluffy powder had already covered the pines—a real fairytale setting. We threw snowballs at each other, tramped through the woods, and returned to the lodge exhilarated and cold. Delighted to see that we would be the only guests for the night, Autumn became frisky and coy. Though we hadn't thought of bringing bathing suits, we decided to take a swim and sauna. I wore

my thin boxer shorts, which became transparent the minute I dove into the water, and Autumn put on my old Harvard T-shirt and her bright red panties.

"After a few laps in the bath-warm pool water, we climbed into the Jacuzzi, which had molded contour seats that accommodated two people. Straddling me, Autumn began tugging at the band of my shorts. So I slipped my hands under her shirt to squeeze her breasts. Through the skylight overhead we could see the snow blowing, the pines dancing in the wind.

" 'I want to make love to you in the pool,' Autumn whispered, pulling my cock free from my shorts. She kissed its head, then jumped away and did a cannonball into the water. I quickly followed, and we were soon locked in a loving embrace with just our heads above the surface. Our underclothes drifted to the pool's bottom. We were soon making love, partially suspended in water as soothing as a womb.

" 'The sauna,' Autumn insisted. So we climbed out dripping and set the sauna to its highest temperature. Inside, we lay side-by-side on the hot wooden planks. 'I want you inside me,' she sighed. Smoothing baby oil over her body, I rubbed a capful between her legs until her mound glistened with oil and sweat. Then I entered her slowly, allowing only the head of my penis to penetrate her upthrust cunt.

" 'Pretend we're not alone,' she whispered. 'Another couple is standing fully clothed outside the window, watching us screw.' The thought of someone observing our performance turned me on, and I began pounding myself against her, yelling for her to tell me when she came.

" 'Fuck me!' she cried. 'Deeper! Faster!' In an instant we climaxed together, laughing and shouting like a couple of kids in their first blizzard. You can

imagine my surprise when we left the sauna and saw a young couple standing nearby, holding hands. We were so covered with sweat, that I blushed and said, 'It's hot in there.' The woman just smiled and said, 'We know!' "

Voyeurism and the Family

How many children have heard strange noises coming from their parents' bedroom late at night and have crept out of bed to peek? Come on, now, be honest. And if you caught a glimpse of what daddy and mommy were doing, did you run straight back to your little bed? You *did?* Come on, now.

Although most of us didn't fully understand what went on before our wondering eyes, we may have found ourselves strangely stimulated. For many women such an experience initiated the popular "getting caught" fantasy wherein they take delight from the thought of their man catching them screwing their mailman. As adults, many men harbor the fantasy of secretly watching their wives or other couples make love.

Barrett goes wild with passion when Jennifer tells him:

"One afternoon, you developed a headache at the office and came home early. Weren't you surprised to see me already in bed but with the boy who cleans our pool! After seeing us, you quickly stepped out of the bedroom and went around to peek in our bedroom window. You loved watching his firm, hard body on top of mine, pumping hard while I wriggled and moaned underneath him. And you became very excited when he stopped fucking me and went down on me, lapping up my pussy juices while I cried out in

ecstasy. When you saw that we were finally finished, you ran back to the garage, backed out of the driveway, drove around the block, and then came home. You then found me in the shower. And unable to wait any longer, since you were so excited over what you had seen earlier, you fucked me harder and hotter than ever before right there on the bathroom floor."

Have you considered voyeurism kinky? Well, if it is the *only* way a man can get off, it may be. But otherwise, it is harmless and exciting—and as American as apple pie. Voyeuristic fantasy stories are the *only* way one should explore the universal and powerful incest taboo. Laryssa's following fantasy story for Derek skillfully wove voyeurism and incest into an unusual bedtime story:

"Just imagine! While you were in college you came home one Easter to meet your sister's brand-new fiancé. Wasn't it wonderful to return to Florida after freezing in Montana for four months?

"The day after Easter, your parents went shopping for the afternoon, leaving just you, your sister, and Jan, her fiancé, at home lying by the pool. You couldn't help but admire your sister's trim figure as she lay sunning herself in a skimpy bikini. And as Jan lathered her body with suntan lotion, you noticed the way his hands lingered near the insides of her thighs. Were you shocked and embarrassed at how exciting you found this? Did you get an erection? Quickly you picked up your towel, holding it in front of you as you excused yourself for a nap.

"After you climbed into bed, still hot and hard, you began to masturbate while thinking of Jan's hands on your sister's thighs. Then you heard the tinkling of laughter and glasses from the patio below. When you peeked from behind the blinds, you caught a glimpse

of your sister reaching into a glass, removing an ice cube, and sliding it down Jan's trunks. Soon both were naked and rubbing ice cubes all over each other's glistening bodies. Then Jan poured some of his drink onto your sister's mound and dove between her legs to slowly lap it up. Your sister's nipples hardened, and you reached for your cock, circling its swollen head with trembling fingers. As you slowly beat off, you watched your sister spin around with her legs spread wide. You felt a jolt of electricity at the sight of her gorgeous pussy framed with curly, red pubic hair. You feasted your eyes, stroking your cock faster and faster, while Jan slid his long smooth cock into your sister's pussy and fucked her furiously. She writhed beneath him for what seemed like hours. The harder Jan pumped, the faster you stroked, until the three of you finally exploded simultaneously."

Playing Dress-up

Did you ever creep into your parents' attic when you were a kid and try on mommy's wedding gown? Did your brother don dad's army uniform to pretend he was "Johnny" marching off to war? Most people have done something like that, even if only on Halloween.

A handsome, urbane gentleman who is Chairman of the Board of a Fortune 500 company looked me straight in the eye the other day and confessed his weakness for ladies' lingerie. This man had played middle linebacker for UCLA, had served as an Admiral in the Navy, and was married to a beautiful and cultured woman. They raised three wonderful children, live in a Tudor mansion, and hold the highest respect of their community. But late at night, with no one but his wife looking, Taylor dolls himself up in a satin negligee from Saks Fifth Avenue, slips into a pair of silk pantyhose, and drenches himself in perfume. On occasion, his wife Patricia will apply makeup to his face and slip a beautiful blond wig over his distinguished gray locks.

While traveling to Boston on business one fall, they heard about the International Fantasia Fair, which attracts hundreds of cross-dressers from all over the world. From a well-written article in *Boston* magazine, Patricia gleaned the fabric for a fantasy that keeps old Taylor forever young in her arms:

"We've just returned from the Fantasia Fair in Provincetown, exhilarated after a wonderful week of dancing and partying. Oh, Taylor, you looked so absolutely ravishing in the black sequined gown you wore the night of the ball, I felt so lucky to be with you! What really made me love you, however, was returning from a sailboat ride to find you lying on the bed in our suite dressed in my mauve silk negligee. Quickly, I disrobed and curled next to you on the bed, rubbing your smooth hard body with mine until I felt you getting hard underneath your gown. I undressed you slowly, until you were naked except for your pantyhose. Leaning over you, I gently blew on your crotch through the pantyhose. That huge cock begged to be set free. But I wanted to relish seeing it strain and throb, so I caressed your balls and licked your cock through the fine fabric as you lay motionless, sighing in delight. After a while, I straddled your body and pulled at your erection still locked into the pantyhose, until I was able to slide the very tip of your cock into me. 'Take it all!', you cried. But I continued to raise and lower my soaking cuntlips over your manhood. Finally, when I knew you had soared near the point of climax, I slipped free your cock and placed your silk

negligee between our bodies so that we could both enjoy the exquisite sensation of rubbing our hot bodies against it. When we finally reached our orgasms, they were the best we had ever had."

Dedicated to Nursing Mothers

Felicia, a very good friend of mine, recently gave birth to a beautiful baby girl. Her husband, Noah, loves to sit with his arm around her stroking her unoccupied breast while baby Jolie sucks her mother's nourishment. Six weeks after Jolie's birth, on the first night the couple could again make love, Felicia wove a fantasy story that drove Noah to drink:

"The other morning while I was nursing Jolie, I had the wildest fantasy that you were in bed with us. After Jolie had sucked her fill and had dozed off, you drew back the covers and joined me in bed, wearing nothing but a loving smile. Slowly you began to fondle my free breast, which delighted me so deeply that I felt the old twinge of excitement in my vagina. When you slowly ran your tongue around my hardened nipple, I soon felt myself getting soaking wet with desire. I stroked your hair and encouraged you to touch my pubic hair, and I grasped your hair in my free hand.

"As Jolie dozed, you began to gently explore me with your fingers and to softly blow on my vagina. Your warm breath sent tingling sensations deep into my womb. And you continued to fondle my free nipple. Since I didn't want to disturb the baby, I tried not to move. But I grew so excited, I invited you to enter me. Gently, you slid your wonderful penis deep inside me, fucking me ever so gracefully so as not to disturb our little doll. I felt myself becoming hotter and hotter, and I struggled against the urge to churn my pelvis, to

meet your slow, gentle rhythm, my heart pounding wildly beneath my breast.

"When Jolie yawned, I feared we'd awakened her. But she continued to doze contentedly with her lips nuzzling my breast. Your hands covered my body, stroked my thighs, and massaged my belly. Then, when you were about to reach your climax, still pumping softly, I guided your lips to my free breast and fed you my love juice. It was the most tender moment we have ever shared, and I shall always cherish it."

Turning the Tables

So far, you have exerted your total command, ruling the fantasy world that you've created for your lover. But no matter how clever and adroit you have grown, you may still have overlooked one or several exquisite treasures. Keep digging for those golden keys. But if you find yourself a little at a loss or tired of excavating clues, don't be afraid to ask your man for help. After creating so many fantasy stories for your man, you can finally feel free to ask for his help. The next time you create a fantasy story for him, pause frequently to ask him his reactions: "Do you like that? How would you change this story?"

EXERCISE 7

Fill in the Blanks

Tell your man that you are going to create a fill-in-the-blanks story and that every time you pause he should volunteer the missing pieces. To effectively enlist his help, let him help you create the script. If he needs a little coaxing, as he probably will, this love game will do the trick:

"Let's make believe that we are on vacation in ______________. When we arrive, we notice ______________ sitting in the lobby. You whisper in my ear that you'd enjoy ______________. That night at dinner I wear ______________. At the next table you see ______________. You suggest ______________. When we get back to our room we both ______________. After we're through I put on ______________. Then we ______________. I begin by ______________ and slowly progress to ______________. You ask me to ______________, and I ______________ until you ______________. When I'm sure that you are almost ______________, I change positions and ______________. Your ______________ feels ______________, and I love it so much that I ______________. Then I let you ______________ to me ______________.

"Suddenly there's a knock on the door and ______________. You reach for your ______________ and I ______________. When you ask if I ______________, I say 'It's up to you.' We proceed to ______________ while you touch ______________ and I touch ______________ with my ______________. Finally, you take me in your ______________ and ______________ me until we both ______________."

EXERCISE 8

Now He's the Director

One night before you've made love and before you have told your man his fantasy story, fish your trusty tape recorder out of your erotic toolbox and ask him to create a fantasy story for himself. If he needs help you can start the tale, quickly relinquishing control to him. If he still needs help, present him with a copy of *Forum* and suggest that he adapt one of its letters, freely changing the names, settings, and action to personalize it. He'll catch on quickly (just as you did, many chapters ago) and will surely reveal something that you've overlooked. Then, the next time you make love, turn on the tape and let him hear himself "talking dirty." You see, many people find it hard to talk in detail during actual lovemaking, which explains why video cassettes have become a popular tool for lovers who want to place themselves in the middle of the action without having to say a word.

Martha, who followed this suggestion, found that her man fantasized about starring in *Rocky.* Now she can turn her man into a prizefighter just by playing the *Rocky* theme during an after-dinner brandy.

LESSON 8

Sequels

Even as I write the last chapter of this book, fantasy stories continue to pour in. Captains of industry, physicians, lawyers, soldiers, and students all express eagerness for their ladies to learn how to whisper. And the women joyfully shout: "It really works!"

One night not long ago I met my agent for a business meeting at a bar in a major convention hotel. While we talked, the manuscript and a manuscript cover photo lay near my elbow. As the bar filled up, a group of distinguished executives sat nearby. Their leader, a white-haired, expensively dressed gentleman of about fifty-five, couldn't take his eyes off the cover photo. Michael, my agent, handed him a chapter to read.

After a few minutes, the gentleman looked up from his reading, shook his head in wonder, and said, "I wish my wife had read this book when we were younger. If she'd do just one thing you suggest, hell, I'd never screw around again! You know, most men would rather share their fantasies with their special women. But my wife was brought up strictly. *You* know what I mean. It would be so much easier for men to be true to their wives if the wives could learn to add a little spice from time to time. Hey, maybe it's not too late. Can you let me know when the book's published?"

This man spoke from his heart, as have many of the men who have shared their fantasies with me. Ryan and I have smoothed the rockier moments of our relationship because we have grown to be each other's best friend. We play together, cry together, fight together, and love together. Yet we never take each other for granted. Of course, I know *his* fantasies and he also knows *mine*. Though we each lead busy lives and encounter new situations and new people every day, we remain unswervingly loyal to one another.

As we grow and learn, we seize every new opportunity for creating even better fantasy stories. Currently, Ryan is building a large addition onto our Cape Cod retreat. The sight of his beautiful body glistening with sweat as he hoists beams and pounds nails has generated a hot new carpenter fantasy. Since he loves my erotic stories, Ryan encourages me by helping detect clues. He insists, "When you first started whispering in my ear, I was afraid you'd taken over my mind! It scared me. Now that I can freely give you clues myself, I've gotten back a certain amount of control. But we finally became two equals in the crazy game of love when *I* learned how to whisper in *your* ear."

Step One: Getting Your Man to Volunteer Clues

If he's like most men, your lover will progress through predictable stages, first growing comfortable with your freshly kindled sexual assertiveness, then looking forward to increasing eroticism, and then actually begging for more. At that point you can encourage him to come right out and tell you exactly what he wants, allowing him to help construct his own dream fantasies. Yvette's lover tapes clues to her birth control pill dispenser, Liz's lover records clues on cassettes, and Martha's man sends her flowers every few weeks with clues neatly printed on the card.

Recently, Martha's sweetheart (remember his *Rocky* fantasy?) telegrammed a dozen red roses with tickets to a championship fight in Las Vegas! On the three subsequent days, she received first-class, round-trip airline tickets, a silver garter belt, and finally a five-hundred dollar gift certificate from an elegant boutique.

Before they left for Nevada, Martha bought a wardrobe tailored to her man's erotic tastes. They held hands on the plane, her man frequently fingering the top of Martha's new sheer black stockings whenever her red silk dress hiked up her leg.

In Las Vegas they sat holding hands while the Champ pulverized his opponent, and her man whispered in *her* ear, "Pretend you're going to bed with *him* tonight!" Surprise! Martha's man had been observant enough to have figured out Martha's own excitement over the prizefighting fantasies she wove. When they got back to the room, Martha delivered the punch:

"*Later tonight, the winner is joining us at* your *invitation! After he gets here, we'll have a few drinks.*

Then you are going to tell him that I give the best 'head' in the world. I'll be sitting at his feet, and I'll get very wet when I see his crotch bulge. Won't he get hard when I suck the olive out of my martini? I'll drop the straps of my white chemise, exposing my breasts while I take off his pants and shorts. When I release his long, thick cock with engorged purple veins, I'll start to salivate. I just can't wait to get my lips around that huge hunk of meat. While you watch, his manhood will fill my mouth—thrusting deeper and deeper down my throat until my lips kiss his balls. On the couch, stroking your own big cock, you'll love it when the Champ starts to come—panting, his head thrown back, his massive fingers tangled in my hair. I'll swallow it all. Imagine me bringing the world's champ to his knees!

"Now it is the challenger's turn. I'll motion you to join on the floor so that the Champ can watch as you fuck me dog-style, my tits swinging wildly while I scream for more. Can you and I go at it for over an hour? The Champ will be amazed by your staying power and will cheer you on, yelling, 'Fuck her for me, Champ!' God, how I'll climax when you finally start to come deep inside my pussy."

Surprisingly, Sandi found it a bit harder to get her lover to volunteer clues. Although the fantasy stories Sandi wove for him gave them both great pleasure, she always felt Dick pull back at the last minute, not quite reaching the ultimate peak she wanted to share with him.

Finally, one night as she tailored a cowboy fantasy, Sandi noticed that Dick continually fondled the life-size replica of a .357 Magnum that she had brought him as a prop since he loved guns. Fantasy stories featuring them always led to fevered lovemaking, with Dick encouraging Sandi to get on top. This particular night, after several perfect Manhattans, Sandi took the toy gun from Dick and pushed the tip of its barrel into her vagina. When Dick sat up to watch, his cock throbbing and his eyes glazing, Sandi asked him what he wanted her to do next. "Rub my gun on your clit," he whispered. "There. Hold it with both hands. Spread your legs wider. Good, baby. That's good." He bent his head close to her crotch and continued.

"We're in a Mexican whorehouse. I've just come back from border patrol. A couple of drug smugglers fired some shots at me, and my gun is still hot from the action. I'm aching to get laid. So I go to my favorite brothel, where I meet you, all decked out in a yellow kimono." Dick shuddered. Sandi lost herself in his story and in the sensation of stroking herself with the toy gun. Soon Dick put his hands on the Magnum and fucked her steadily as he continued his story. "You loved law enforcement officers, with their big guns and wicks. And you asked to play with my still-warm automatic. I showed you how to fire it. Then you climbed on top of me, screwing and squealing, firing round after round into the ceiling. I came like a battering ram that night."

Through her mounting orgasm, Sandi picked up this precious clue and scrambled on top of Dick, yelling, "Shoot me with your come, soldier!" She waved the toy pistol frantically. "Bang me, baby. Bang me fast and deep. Bang me!" Dick bucked wildly, then came in a body-wrenching climax, his cock throbbing in Sandi's pussy as never before.

"It's funny," confesses Sandi, "but that night I got even more turned on than he did."

Yvette, on the other hand, marveled at her lover's creativity and encouraged him to continue telling stories until they each settled comfortably into alternately creating fantasies for one other. Nevertheless,

Yvette still sensed that her man, Drake, was holding something back. "I was so persistent," she writes. "And one time I came as close as I think I'll ever come." Noticing that Drake admired Angie Dickinson on "Police Woman," Yvette tried out this story:

"One night while you were driving your Cadillac home after an out-of-state business trip, you were feeling so grimy that you stopped at a laundromat at 1:00 A.M. to freshen up. You took off all your clothes except your tight jockey shorts and threw everything into a washing machine. While you walked to the men's room, you heard a husky female voice yell, 'Freeze! Put your hands over your head, pervert!' You froze. 'Turn around. Slow,' she commanded.

"When you turned you saw a uniformed lady cop pointing a blue-barreled police special at your chest. She had an odd smile on her face. Holding her gun steady, she moved slowly over to you and started to frisk you. 'You got a concealed weapon in there, buster?' she asked when she saw the bulge in your shorts. 'Pull your pants down. And no monkey business either.' She was short, about fifteen pounds shy of chunky, and the sight of her big round breasts stretching her uniform turned you on. Your cock throbbed in your shorts, then stood at attention when you pulled them down. She lowered her gun and licked her lips. 'Is that thing loaded?' she asked, and you realized this might be more than a bust for indecent exposure.

" 'My identification is in my car,' you said.

" 'Fuck the identification, buster. I know your type.' Ordering you to lock the front door, she removed her holster, still holding her gun, and unbuttoned her blue blouse. 'You gonna stand there shaking like a dog or are you gonna fuck me?'

"Finally she put her gun down and swiftly pulled off her uniform. You were surprised to see she wore no underwear. Her body was firm and compact, her legs and arms muscular, her tits and ass large and inviting. When she lowered her head over your throbbing cock, she moved her tongue up and down the shaft, murmuring and sucking it like a lollipop. Before you could explode in her mouth, she stood back and said, 'Don't forget who's in charge here!'

"Then she ordered you to kneel in front of her so you could count the hairs on her gorgeous black pussy. You could see a trickle of love juices dribbling down her thighs. 'Ever eat a cop?' she asked, pushing your face into her cunt and rubbing your nose against her clit. The smell of her cunt intoxicated you as she twisted her hips back and forth, your tongue darting in and out of her cunt. When you nibbled her clit, she wound her fingers in your hair and ground your head against her pelvic bone. Sliding your tongue as far as it would go, you drank her love juice. 'Bite my clit,' she sighed. 'Fingerfuck me!' After one shuddering climax, she pushed you away and lay on the laundry folding table with her legs spread wide. 'Get my night stick,' she commanded. 'And my gun. Don't worry, it's not loaded!'

"While you eased the two-foot long rod in and out of her wet center, she caressed your balls and cock with the cold blue metal of her police special. Every once in a while she would lick the gun's barrel and tenderly suck it as if it were your cock. The night stick became slick with her juices. She had the deepest cunt you'd ever seen. You longed to fuck her every way imaginable, but you remembered what she'd said about being the boss, so you held back.

"Eventually she rolled over, crying, 'Fuck your cop,

baby. Fuck her hard and deep.' You didn't hesitate, but thrust deeply into her dog-style. She started to pant like a locomotive, turning her head back to French kiss you, sticking her hard, round ass high in the air. 'Fuck the dog-cop, you bastard,' she screamed. She wanted it bad. She wanted it fast. She wanted it slow and soft. You obeyed every command. Your balls slapping against her butt, you pounded furiously, then pumped slow-motion. Faster. Slower. Deeper, Softer. Suddenly you were both coming, both your juices running down her legs.

"After you finished, she climbed back into her uniform, strapped on her holster and said, 'This is your lucky night, buster. I'm letting you off for good behavior.' "

Joanna unwittingly taught her latest lover how to whisper in *her* ear during one of her early fantasy stories. She began whispering in the bathroom after getting turned on while watching him shave:

"The other day, I watched you shaving, remembering how when I was a little girl I used to watch my daddy.

"After you left for the office I went to our bed, where my mind soon began to wander. I dreamed you were carefully trimming your mustache after your morning shower. And the sight of you standing there naked and the smell of your cologne got me very horny. I stood in the bathroom doorway wearing nothing but my red baby-doll pajamas. As I watched you clip your whiskers, I began to rub my clit, knowing you could see me juicy for action.

"You scooped me in your arms and carried me to our rumpled bed as I whispered in your ear, 'I love you, Daddy.' 'Are you Daddy's little girl?' you asked

as you twirled my nipples between your fingers. 'Ooh, yes, Daddy, I am your little girl,' I answered.

"Just then you gazed upon my bushy pubic hair and told me that I didn't look like a little girl, but like a full-grown woman. 'Daddy, please make me look like a little girl again,' I teased.

"Rushing back into the bathroom, you retrieved your scissors and returned to find me spreading the lips of my creaming cunt. You quickly trimmed my pussy hair with your mustache scissors, my curly locks falling away to fully expose my mound. Then you squirted mentholated shaving cream into your hand and began lathering my cunt."

Philip thrust his tongue down her throat, devouring her mouth. Then before Joanna could continue her fantasy story, Philip whispered, "The cool cream coated the burning lips of your pussy and you cried out in girlish delight." Philip then pushed his fingers deep into Joanna's dripping cunt. "I took my razor and began carefully shaving your mound, leaving nothing but a tender, soft patch of smooth pink baby skin," he said.

By now Joanna was churning her pelvis in an exquisitely abandoned dance, hanging on his every word. Philip continued, "Then I placed a hot towel on your burning cunt, which began to heave like a volcano. You had never bucked so hard or gotten so slick between your legs, and I felt the startling convulsions of your powerful orgasm. I was almost afraid your cunt would strangle my cock if I put it inside you, so I positioned myself between your legs and began to gently blow on it. 'Fuck me,' you begged. But I smiled and continued to blow. 'Fuck me, hard, Philip!' you cried again, writhing like an animal in heat. Slowly I flicked my tongue across your clit, feeling it harden *and stretch until it seemed you had grown your own cock. Slowly I pushed one finger inside you with my thumb prodding your swollen clit.*

"Unable to stand it any longer, you rolled me over and thrust yourself upon my cock, rocking back and fucking me like a dynamo. How did it feel when my hot come shot into your womb?"

What about your man? Well, you'll never know until you ask! If your man insists that you've left nothing out, that you've driven him to ultimate sexual satisfaction, he may be telling the truth. Let well enough alone.

On the other hand, if he's still shy or has deeply buried his secrets, perhaps you should leave them buried. He may have coupled them with such pain and shame that revealing them might bring nothing but hurt or guilt into your bed. Respect a man's right to privacy, to keep a piece of himself sacred and free for only himself.

Nevertheless, keep a sharp lookout for fresh clues and try to get him talking in bed. If he does start talking, you will be able to move on to the beauty of whispers in your *own* ear.

Step Two: He Feeds Your Fantasies

At the end of this chapter you will find a special game based on the Sexual Fantasy Inventory that will help your man learn *your* secret fantasies. However, before you play it with him you'll want to consider the ways in which men and women differ with respect to erotic talk.

Remember the song in which the woman yearns for a "slow lover with a slow hand"? If your lover hasn't mastered foreplay and mindplay, why do you stay with him? "He's a nice man, holds a good job, and stays faithful," you say. Those traits are fine. But don't you want it *all*?

Even if the man in your life seems totally uncreative, you can still teach him to create fantasy stories for you. If he has responded enthusiastically to your wild and woolly bedtime stories, he's probably already groping for ways to please you. If he's direct and to-the-point, he may actually ask you to confide your fantasies. But if he's like most men, he'll take a little coaxing.

Of course, we women are delightfully more complex and interesting than our men. While our men may appreciate the little thoughtful touches like candlelight and transparent negligee, we, on the other hand, positively revel in them. If a man gets turned on simply by seeing a naked centerfold in *Playboy*, a woman will imagine a lush setting and will leisurely linger in foreplay over a gorgeous hunk in *Playgirl*. And whereas a man will get off in mere minutes while making love, we women prefer to take our time, slowly and lovingly building to our spine-shattering climaxes.

So many differences exist between the males and females of the species that I could write at least one whole book on the subject. But since I don't have room here to do the topic justice, I'll have to settle for a brief introduction to teaching our men how to plumb the labyrinths of female joy. We can get them started with a few simple tricks to:

Loosen Their Tongues

After you've told your man a few fantasy stories you will want to change the pace, returning to the more old-fashioned, straight sex that dominated your earlier relationship. Plan a rather conventional evening: a quiet dinner, perhaps a little dancing, and a nightcap of brandy. While the night's still young, tell him that you're tired but want to make love before you fall asleep. Back home, undress quickly, joining him in bed. Kiss his lips and face, nestle your breasts against his chest, gently blow in his ear. Once he mounts you, pull his head close to yours and whisper, "How does it feel?"

If he's like most men, he'll say something like, "It feels good." But don't let him off the hook.

YOU: "No. I mean, how does it feel to be inside me?"

HE: "It feels great!" [How imaginative!]

YOU: "I like the way you feel inside me. How do I feel?"

HE: "You feel warm and wet." [Progress.]

YOU: "What feels warm and wet?"

HE: "Your insides."

YOU: "My cunt?" [He'll probably thrust more fiercely at this word.]

HE: "Your cunt feels great."

YOU: "Tell me how your cock feels."

HE: "It feels great!" [I didn't say it would be easy, did I?]

YOU: "Tell me how your cock feels in my cunt."

HE: "My cock tingles in your cunt. I could fuck you all night." [Now we're getting somewhere!]

YOU: "I want you to fuck me all night. Fuck me!"

HE: "I love fucking you, baby."

YOU: "Fuck me faster, deeper. Fuck me!"

Now he'll probably come quickly, then roll over and fall asleep leaving you to wonder why men find it so hard to talk sexy in more than monosyllables.

Now, don't be discouraged. Because you have achieved an important, if subtle, breakthrough by giving your man permission to talk dirty to you. That achievement will let you take the next step, revealing to him:

Your Own Sexual Fantasy Inventory

Have you ever gotten turned on while flipping through a calendar such as *Buns*, which displays nude male asses? Do you find your eyes drifting to the crotch of a lithe male dancer in a leotard? Have you ever found yourself getting wet while watching the sex scene in a movie? Well, you can freely reveal these turn-ons to your man, provided you balance your comments by always insisting that your man is bigger, better, and more skillful. After all, you don't want him to feel jealous, to think you find another more attractive, or that you might stray into a new bed.

Perhaps you managed to slip your key into the lock of your own fantasy box the night you gave him permission to talk dirty to you, but now you want him to turn the key to let the lid fly off. After a few more of your own fantasy stories designed to feed *his* fantasies, you might create another conventional evening, this time including an erotic event which stimulates *you* even more than him. For example, imagine you've taken him to the opera to see a new and sensual production of Wagner's *Tristan and Isolde*. After the final curtain falls, you visit a dark, romantic bar where you confess that you got very excited when the muscular Tristan made love to Isolde. In fact, you wondered what it would feel like to make love to your man onstage before the eyes of an appreciative audience. "I bet we could win a standing ovation," you say, lowering your eyes demurely.

Take him home early again, but this time have some

props ready: a rich, stereo recording of *Tristan and Isolde,* a gauzy gown similar to the heroine's, and perhaps a fur mantle for your man. Set the stage carefully with candles around your bed; the music pulsating in the background, a seductive smile on your lips. Tonight's pillowtalk might sound something like this:

YOU: 'I've never wanted you so badly." [You slip your gown off your shoulders to reveal your naked breasts, touching his crotch and squeezing lightly.]

HE: "Me too."

YOU: "What do you want?"

HE: "I want to fuck you."

YOU: "I want you to eat me first, forever. I want to feel your tongue in my pussy. . . . How does it taste?"

HE: "It tastes good." [Oops, he's just lost his tongue again, though in honorable service.]

YOU: "Does my pussy taste salty or sweet?"

HE: "You taste a little bitter. I like to push my tongue into your pussy and suck your pussy lips between my teeth." [Now he's beginning to roll!]

YOU: "Talk to me. Tell me everything."

HE: "You're so beautiful. Did I ever tell you that you have perfect tits, a juicy cunt? I love to feel your mouth on my cock. Suck me."

YOU: "You have such a big cock. I love to feel it throb in my throat. . . . Fuck me now."

HE: "Fuck me, baby. Push your cunt up high. Fuck me, fuck me, fuck me . . ."

Chances are he'll be able to come twice this night. The next morning you can hand him *your* Sexual Fantasy Inventory.

A BRIEF PEEK AT WHISPER IN HER *EAR*

VISUALS

1. The most passionate love scene in a movie you have ever witnessed ______________________.
2. The sexiest thing you have watched a man do to himself ______________________.
3. The sexiest thing you have watched a man do with a woman ______________________.

SENSORY

1. The kind of music that best sets the mood for love ______________________.
2. You prefer a [check one]:
   - _____ soft touch
   - _____ medium touch
   - _____ strong, firm touch
3. The most sensitive parts of your body are:
   - _____ your neck
   - _____ behind your ears
   - _____ your eyelashes
   - _____ your lips
   - _____ your breasts
   - _____ your nipples
   - _____ behind your knees
   - _____ inside your thighs
   - _____ your vagina
   - _____ your toes
   - _____ your ankles
4. The sounds you most respond to while making love are ______________________.

HEROINES

1. The most beautiful woman in the world is ________
________.
2. The part of your body you are most proud of
________.
3. The part of your body you don't want to talk about
________.
4. The kind of woman you wish you could be ________
________.
5. You would like to be described as being sexually
________.
6. Your fantasy woman would lead the kind of life
________.

WHISPERS

1. When participating in foreplay you wish your lover would say ________.
2. At the moment of penetration you wish your lover would say ________.
3. You wish your lover would ask you to ________
________.
4. You hope your lover will tell you that he needs you to ________.

OLD FLAMES

1. The boy you wished you'd made love with ________
________.
2. The high school hunk ________.
3. If you could have played it differently with ________ ________ you would have ________.
4. You would love to receive roses and a love letter from ________.

LOVEMAKING

1. The position you'd love to try while making love ______________________________.
2. The position that would be the naughtiest ______________________________.
3. The position that brings you quickly to orgasm ______________________________.
4. You wish your lover would spend more time ______________________________.
5. You wish your lover would spend less time ______________________________.

POSSESSIONS

1. More than anything in the world you would like to own ______________________________.
2. Your favorite jewel is ______________________________.
3. Your favorite fur is ______________________________.
4. Your dream house would look like ______________________________.
5. The best collection you could own would be ______________________________.

Confiding Your Deepest, Darkest Secrets

How many times have you heard the sage advice to retain an air of mystery? Don't worry, teaching your man to create fantasy stories for you will increase, rather than detract from, your mysteriousness. As his curiosity is continually aroused, you can become even more unpredictable, whimsical, and bewitching. Just when he thinks that he has unraveled your deepest, darkest secrets you can bestow a clue to yet a deeper layer, keeping him perenially intrigued.

Martha, Sammy Jo, and Yvette have all trained their men to bewitch them, without sacrificing their mystique.

Martha's lover has discovered that Martha longed to be a high school cheerleader on the arm of the captain of the basketball team. So every so often he weaves her a wonderful fantasy story complete with megaphone and pom-poms.

Cary has entered shapely Sammy Jo in a dozen wet T-shirt contests, if only in her dreams. Of course, she always wins. Acting out her exhibitionist fantasy, Sammy Jo finally did enter such a contest and beat out ten nubile teenagers for the title. Cary happily displays the trophy and her picture to his running buddies.

And bold, beautiful Yvette? Nothing makes her happier than to have her "daddy" tell her that she's a naughty girl as she revels in a fantasy orgy at a nude beach. And was Yvette wrong to tell her lover Drake that she has wanted to fuck Santa Claus ever since she was a little girl? Not at all. "Have you ever been eaten out by a guy with a soft white beard?" she laughs. And the beat goes on.

These happy couples have built lasting relationships that never lose their treasured spice. As with any treasure, they handle their fantasy lives discreetly and carefully, treating them with care and saving them for special occasions. Don't you reserve the Baccarat crystal for company? Much of the time these couples depend on predictable and reliable, straight, tender, loving sex. But just when the going gets too smooth and easy, one or the other person will cuddle up close, engage the loved one's eyes, and softly, sexily, sweetly, and seductively whisper in the other's ear.

Real Women Love Flowers, Chocolates, and Mushy Cards

Born with her rich female imagination, any woman can dream she serves a Greek tycoon, shines as a prima ballerina, plays a goddess on the silver screen, or bounds across the surface of the moon. Regardless of the images in her head, however, every woman demands love and romance—in that order. The need to love and be loved powers a woman's life. Whether a man conveys the message through a special gift, a tender gesture, or the words themselves, he'll always find "I love you" to be the perfect preamble to passionate sex.

Every woman wants to feel desirable, to be able to drive a man's hands and lips out of control. She spends hours selecting her perfume, considering how to style her hair, and which dress to wear. Her man should reinforce her good judgment, particularly when creating fantasy stories. Little clues to your man will help tremendously. For instance, if he says he loves your perfume, ask him to dab a little between your legs the next time you make love. If he says he'd love to see you in a corset and garters, tell him to pick them out in his favorite color.

My beloved Ryan can eventually tease me away

from my typewriter by wooing me with a bouquet of flowers bought on his way home from the hospital after work. And if he has tucked a little love note into the bouquet, he can tease me all the way into the bedroom. When the little note says, "Forget you're a writer and remember you're a hot-blooded woman," it will make me forget trying to untangle a troublesome sentence.

Initially, Ryan's love notes sounded like weak valentines—"Sweets for the sweet" and "Hugs and kisses"—until I whispered, "Write me a note that tells me *exactly* what you want to do in bed." The next day he sprang a bouquet of daisies on me with a note saying, "Let's fuck in the sunlight." Encouraged, I asked him to describe what our lovemaking would be like on a deserted beach. Looking a little sheepish, he said, "I can't talk and make love at the same time."

"Then tell me the story first, then we'll make love!" I said.

"We are at the nude beach at five o'clock. So no one else is in sight. Your tits are brown and lovely. When you see my hard-on you insist I make love to you in broad daylight. . . . It was fun."

"Fun?" I pouted. "But what *exactly* did we do?"

"Aw, you know," he said blushing deeply. Since he obviously felt embarrassed and afraid of disappointing me, I decided to drop the idea for a few days. The night's lovemaking was a little clumsy because he seemed to have momentarily lost a little self-confidence.

Three days later I tried a new approach to teaching my old dog a new trick. This time I began cautiously taking the time to embrace him and cover him with tiny kisses as we lay naked on our bed. "Let's play a little game," I encouraged, reassuringly holding his hand. "Let me teach you something about my body that no one learns in medical school." Ryan's scientific curiosity took over, and he moved closer to me. I continued, "I want you to say certain words or phrases. My body will automatically signal whenever you push one of my erotic buttons."

Eager for any new game, Ryan agreed. Quickly, I rolled over to lie on my belly, arms at my side, knees pressed tightly together.

"Do I get some clues?" he asked.

"Let's pretend you've just met me and I'm only nineteen," I answered, still motionless.

"You have wonderfully mature breasts for nineteen. . . . And you have just won a beauty contest—you're the Seafood Goddess," he began. [He knew I had been in several beauty contests while in high school.] "Mmm," I murmured, wiggling slightly to encourage him.

"I am a cadet at the Maritime Academy and have been fixed up to be your blind date for the evening." I remained silent and still.

"After a formal reception, I offer to drive you home in my convertible. You love the way the wind whips through your dress as I speed along the highway. Instead of taking you straight home, I invite you to the top of Cadillac Mountain to see the view under the starlight."

I spread my legs just a tiny bit. Hadn't I once confessed that I coveted our neighbor's new red Mercedes convertible?

"We sat there on top of the mountain watching the moonlight dance across the waves a thousand feet below. We began to kiss passionately, exploring each other's mouths with our tongues, until I finally rested my hand lightly on your breasts," Ryan went on.

I spread my legs a little wider and emitted a long, sweet sigh. Ryan began to kiss the backs of my knees, making me moan as he nipped my buttocks. Tracing a path down the inside of my thighs with his fingertips, he could surely see my toes had begun to curl.

He continued, "Suppose your boyfriend knew what you were letting me do to you."

I turned over, careful to keep my legs closed.

"Soon I unzippered your gown and toyed with your ripe nipples, which swelled beneath my touch."

Ryan pointed at my stiffening nipple and chuckled. I knew he was enjoying the fantasy story as much as I was.

"Soon I peeled off your gown so I could see you naked except for your garter belt and silk stockings. Naked in the moonlight, you looked so beautiful and sexy that I felt myself falling madly in love."

Goose bumps slowly crept over my body.

"Then, for the first time in your life you felt a man's hand caress your virgin pussy, which turned hot and slick in an instant. That delighted me."

My nipples were hard as raisins, the goose bumps blossomed, and I spread my legs a little more. By now, Ryan had a full erection.

"I massaged your pussy until my hands dripped with your juices, and you begged me to slide a finger slowly inside you. Though you recoiled slightly when I penetrated the tight opening, you urged me to go deeper. I could feel your tight hymen vibrating against my fingernail, so I pushed it ever so gently. Fighting free of my school uniform, I poised my hard penis at the mouth of your sex and struggled to enter you, careful not to hurt you too much. You bucked up suddenly, sucking the full shaft to its hilt without even a cry of pain."

While he talked, Ryan slid two fingers into my

soaking-wet pussy until my pelvis was gyrating frantically.

"God, but you're lovely," he said huskily. I looked at him with adoration in my eyes, silently telling him how safe I felt responding to him while he probed my secret fantasies. He soon stopped talking and began making slow, exquisite, passionate love to me.

When we finished almost an hour later, a new, deeper tenderness had evolved between us. Cradling my head in his arms, Ryan studied my face for a long time with a look I can only describe as pure, selfless love. "Thank you for loving me," he said. I kissed his lips. "Just one question, Liane. When did you really fall in love with me?" Although I didn't even have to think about my answer, I pretended to ponder the question before answering, "That very first time, when I whispered in your ear."

EXERCISE 9

The Whisper in His Ear Game

You'll need:
- Three dice
- "His" and "Her" gameboards for each player (plain paper or sturdy poster board)
- Pencils

Rule off eighteen slots to make your gameboard

You can fill in the eighteen slots with any directions you like, from mild to hot. For example:

Whisper in His Ear—Her Gameboard

Silly	*Autoerotic*	*Foreplay*
1 get on all fours	2 pretend you're eating ice cream	3 touch an erotic zone on yourself
4 imitate a wolf in heat	5 take off one piece of clothing	6 touch your host in an erotic zone
7 get in your dog or cat's favorite position	8 rub your ass against your host	9 rub ice cubes on your nipples
10 pretend you're Marilyn Monroe	11 take off your skirt or slacks	12 tickle your pussy with a feather
13 lap milk out of a saucer	14 strip to your undies	15 read aloud from *Forum*
16 recite a nursery rhyme	17 hold a piece of fruit between your breasts	18 masturbate

Rules: roll the dice, total the score, and find the corresponding number on the board. Take it from there. If you dare, you can advance the headings to "Foreplay," "Intercourse," and "Group Sex."

Whisper in Her Ear—His Gameboard

Silly	*Autoerotic*	*Foreplay*
1 sing a love song to your date	2 take off your pants	3 give your date a bath
4 do three ballet steps	5 recite a poem, to the hostess's crotch	6 describe the last night's lovemaking
7 pretend you're a rock singer	8 strip to your shorts	9 moon the crowd
10 lie on the floor and shake your bum	11 walk around the room with a banana between your legs	12 run a feather across the pussy of your date
13 do a belly dance	14 touch your date's nipples	15 eat ice cream out of her mouth
16 put on the hostess's blouse	17 lick your girlfriend's neck and behind her knees	18 masturbate

Would you like to share your special fantasy stories with the author? She'd love to hear from you. Mail your fantasy stories in complete confidence to:

Liane Gardner
Drawer X
Truro, Massachusetts 02666

THE BOOK OF HEROIC FAILURES

Stephen Pile

'Are you fed up with all those books telling you how to be successful? Are you dreadful at most things you try? Here at long last is a book in praise of spectacular failure and people who can't do a thing'
Namib Times

'One of the few books to make me laugh out loud'
Sunday Express

'One of the funniest and most entertaining books I have dipped into for a long time'
Country Life

'(A) splendid panorama of non-achievement'
Sunday Telegraph

'As a serious book it's a failure, as a tonic to make your ribs ache, it's a rip-roaring success'
Manchester Evening News

'A disaster'
Stephen Pile

Futura Publications
Non-Fiction
0 7088 1908 7

THE HENRY ROOT LETTERS

Henry Root

UNIVERSAL ACCLAIM FOR THE LITERARY MASTERPIECE OF THE DECADE!

'One of the funniest books I have ever read'
Auberon Waugh, *Private Eye*

'About as funny as pushing somebody fully clothed into a swimming pool'
Lynda Lee-Potter, *Daily Mail*

'A brave publishing venture' *Books and Bookmen*

'The letters in themselves are of absolutely no interest'
The Spectator

'Very funny' *Punch*

'A deplorable work . . . a disgrace to publishing'
London Review of Books

'If I found some of them difficult to read, it was only because of tears of laughter'
Colin Welch, *Daily Telegraph*

'Uninspiring' *Southend and District Standard*

'We probably won't see a funnier book published this year' Tony Davies, *The Observer*

'Embarrassing' *Irish Times*

'It deserves to be bought by all who know a laugh when they see one' Basil Boothroyd, *The Times*

'A valid contribution, in my opinion, to the great debate' Henry Root, *Henry Root Wet Fish Ltd.*

Futura Publications
Humour
0 7088 1888 9

HENRY ROOT'S WORLD OF KNOWLEDGE

From the man who brought you the immortal LETTERS

Everything you thought you knew about everything – the first and most comprehensive one-volume encyclopaedia of British common sense ever to be published, covering the *Complete* A to Z from Ablutions to God to Overeating and Zoroaster:

★ Authoritative
★ Up-to-date
★ Readable
★ Clear and concise
★ Animals
★ Things
★ 9 Antelopes
★ 11,000 facts
★ 430 definitions

A world of knowledge in a nutshell

'A triumph for common sense'
Times Literary Supplement

Futura Publications
Non-Fiction
0 7088 2329 7